Susan Lusk / Mark Gabor

111 Shops
in New York
That You
Must Not Miss

emons:

Bibliographical Information of the Deutsche Nationalbibliothek
The Deutsche Nationalbibliothek lists this publication
in the Deutsche Nationalbibliografie; detailed bibliographical
data are available on the internet at http://dnb.d-nb.de

© Emons Verlag GmbH
All rights reserved
Design: TIZIAN BOOKS, based on a design
by Lübbeke / Naumann / Thoben
All photos © Susan Lusk except: Amorino Gelato by Amorino Gelato; Laura
Lobdell by Marc Yankus; Metropolitan Museum Store (top) by Metropolitan
Museum Store; Tisane Pharmacy (top) by Jo-Anne Elikann; Vintage Thrift Shop
by Vintage Thrift. Casa de las Velas original painting by Bordoñez.
Editing: Monika E. Schurr
Typesetting and digital processing: Gerd Wiechcinski
Maps / Cartography: altancicek.design, www.altancicek.de
Maps based on data by Openstreetmap, © Openstreet Map-participants, ODbL
Printing and binding: B.O.S.S Medien GmbH, Goch
Printed in Germany 2015
ISBN 978-3-95451-351-2
Revised third edition, November 2015

Did you enjoy it? Do you want more?
Join us in uncovering new places around the world on:
www.111places.com

Foreword

From Afghanistan to Zimbabwe, New York is home to hundreds of different cultures. In its midst are communities like Little Italy and Chinatown, churches of every faith, thousands of 'foreign' restaurants, and of course an endless variety of specialized shops.

New York has its own historical identity and character, evolved over the centuries through a steady flow of immigrants from every continent. It is easily the most international city in the world and is still the world's largest melting pot. It is at once elegant, squalid, playful, serious, ambitious, mundane, and full of *attitude*.

Owing to the vast cultural mix, New York shops are surely the most varied. From buttons to rare books, from penny-candy to priceless artifacts, we have something to satisfy every taste and desire.

The only constant in New York is change. Old neighborhoods morph into hip enclaves. The once-renowned Orchard Street – with over a century of pushcart bargains vended by generations of immigrant Jews – is virtually gone, replaced by some of the city's trendiest boutiques, bars, restaurants, and clubs. Chelsea, once a working-class area, is now a gentrified hub for New York's gay population, and also the hottest center for art galleries.

Likewise, the shops are ever changing – from shoe stores to sushi bars, from textile shops to nail salons, from pharmacies to galleries. Take a two-week vacation and when you return there are two new stores down the street!

Our book can only scratch the surface as a shopper's paradise. For every one of the 111 entries, a dozen were discarded. The choices seemed endless. In the end, we went for the widest variety – the most unusual or unexpected, quirky or offbeat, the most specialized, stylish, funky, obvious (a few), or obscure. But above all, we tried to capture the reader's imagination with the most fascinating shops in New York City.

Let's do it!

111 Shops

1 ABC Carpet & Home
You're not in Kansas anymore

You know that magical moment in *The Wizard of Oz* when Dorothy, living in a black-and-white world, opens her front door and for the first time sees a world of brilliant, dazzling color? That's what it's like to step from the gray granite canyon of the Flatiron District into this vast, sparkling emporium. It almost takes your breath away.

Led by your senses, meander through the main floor's archipelago of scintillating displays: themed home decor is juxtaposed with designer jewelry; islands of alluring fragrance and apothecary dot the aisles near a forest of soft-glowing lighting solutions. ABC Carpet & Home is not simply a showroom – it's a transformative shopping experience incorporating theater, education, food, and art. Beauty and magic are seamlessly blended in a richly textured environment bursting with endlessly tasteful and useful products – a store that advances the notion of *home as sacred space*. This is the essence of the store's retail philosophy, offering "choice at the cutting edge of design and sustainability to create a home as an expression of individual vision and values."

Started as a one-man pushcart business selling remnants of used carpets and linoleum in the 1890s, ABC has emerged as the largest carpet and home furnishings store in the world. Seven floors of furniture and decor fill the main building, the top floor devoted entirely to designer and decorative handmade rugs; the annex across the street sells only carpets and rugs. Newer forays reach into high-end apparel and food, providing holistic, homeopathic, and sustainable lifestyle choices.

Take a break from shopping at either of the two celebrated restaurants tucked at the far end of the ground floor: ABC Kitchen and ABC Cocina, featuring cuisine by a Michelin star chef. This is, indeed, one of the more evolved, sophisticated stores in the city, maybe on the planet. You've landed in Oz.

Address 888 Broadway (at 19th Street), New York 10003, Phone +1 212.473.3000, www.abchome.com, info@abchome.com | Transit Subway: 14 St-Union Sq (L, N, Q, R), Union Sq (4, 5, 6); 23 St (N, R), Bus: M1, M2, M3, M5, M14, M23 | Hours Mon–W Fri–Sat 10am–7pm, Thurs 10am–8pm, Sun 12–6pm

2 A&J Lingerie & More

Tickle your fancy in an un-fancy store

You could easily miss the steps of the nondescript brownstone leading you one flight up to what an erotic guide dubbed "New York's Best Kept Secret." According to owner Jimi Bure, the steps are an important barrier because they discourage undesirables who would wander in off the street just to get kicks ogling sexy paraphernalia. Jimi believes in healthy boundaries – he'll throw out anyone who is disrespectful or otherwise sleazy.

He's a family man, after all. And the proof is, he works full-time everyday with his mother Ida, a nurturing, energetic Latina woman with a handful of candy kisses for any customer she favors. Adding to the family atmosphere is a demure niece who serves clients in the front end of the store, where bubblegum-pink walls are lined end-to-end with 'naughty-wear' for every taste, in every color, and in all sizes, including Plus. Most garments are one-size-fits-all and worn just for fun. As Ida points out with a wink, "They usually don't stay on for long."

The rear of the shop is Jimi's domain – sex toys, which are responsible for seventy percent of A&J's business. You'll find playthings from the expected to the exotic: vibrators/pulsators/bullets/dildos, sex games, videos, erotic party favors and novelties, like penis-shaped cookie-cutters.

A&J didn't start out this way. At first it was a typical neighborhood shop selling ladies' fashions. As business dwindled in the nineties, Jimi reasoned that "what always sells, in good or hard times, is drugs, alcohol, and sex." So he and mama Ida opened an affordable sexy lingerie outlet. Response was great, and the clientele, mostly women, increasingly asked for adult novelties.

When you combine the merchandise with three generations of onsite staff, you have a unique environment – welcoming, relaxed, respectful, safe, but most of all, fun. Nothing uppity. No pressure to buy. And prices that cannot be beat. This is a family affair.

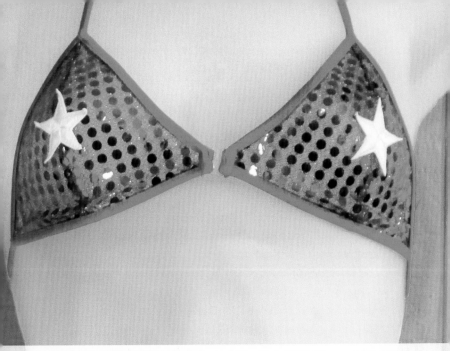

Address 41 West 28 Street (near Sixth Avenue), New York 10001, Phone +1 212.779.1141, www.ajlingerie.com, lingerienyc@hotmail.com | Transit Subway: 28 St (N, R, 1, 6); 34 St-Herald Sq (B, D, F, M, Q), Bus: M1, M2, M3, M4, M5, M7, M20, M23, M34 | Hours Mon–Fri 10am–7pm, Sat 10am–5pm

3_Amorino Gelato

A rose is a rose is a ... gelato!

When you're in the mood for a literally beautiful treat, head to Amorino in the Village for an ice cream cone artfully crafted into an elegant, edible flower. Skilled servers sculpt the creamy gelato into the shape of a large blossoming rose, where each delectable petal can be a different flavor of your choice (Brazilian passion fruit, burnt salted caramel, and cinnamon-spiked Belgian speculoos are among the many temptations). Design your own lickable treat with some of the most inventive flavors imaginable, savoring as many of their twenty-odd choices as you'd like to taste at one time!

Amorino's artisanal gelato is freshly made daily by trained chefs, in small batches and using only organic and natural ingredients – never artificial flavors or colors – churned together in the authentic Italian tradition. Besides ice creams, sorbets, and granitas (fine-shaved ices), they serve traditional Italian focaccina (an eggy brioche filled with gelato), waffles and crepes topped with gelato or warm chocolate sauce, a choice of rich coffees and Italian sodas, plus cakes, gourmet chocolates, truffles, and other mouthwatering Italian confections.

This European-based enterprise, created by two Italian boyhood friends, has over fifty *gelaterias* worldwide. The University Place location is America's flagship store, with a warm and inviting neo-Renaissance atmosphere that attracts a daily mix of sweets-lovers: parents with kids after school, locals meeting for coffee, tourists on a sightseeing break, congregating NYU students, couples out on a date. They enjoy their desserts in an old world ambience – on leather banquettes or in comfy chairs by the faux fireplace, complete with frolicking cherubs and mellow music. *Amorino* means little angel, which is the company's logo, and refers to "the cupid that makes you fall in love with our gelato."

So get the real scoop, and go pluck yourself some petals!

Address 60 University Place (at 10th Street), New York 10003, Phone +1 212.253.5599, www.amorino.com, ny@amorino.com | Transit Subway: 14 St-Union Sq (4, 5, 6, Q, L); 8 St-NYU (N, R); West 4 St (A, B, C, D, E, F, M), Bus: M1, M2, M3, M5, M8, M14, M102, M103 | Hours Sun–Thurs 11am–11pm, Fri–Sat 11am–12am

4 Amy's Bread
Rising to the occasion

Amy's Bread challenges the biblical notion that "man cannot live by bread alone." The art of baking has been elevated to new levels of excellence – crusty, hearth-baked breads and select sweets emerge from their ovens daily and are among the finest to be found anywhere in New York. There are three locations in Manhattan: the original in Hell's Kitchen with a small cafe, Chelsea Market (also offering thin-crust pizzas), and Greenwich Village.

Amy's embraces the best of traditional European baking methods along with a high-consciousness connection to their customers, community, and employees – whom they consider "our baking family." Amy's goal is "to create a bakery and cafe that nourishes the body, mind, and spirit by making carefully hand-crafted foods that taste as good as they look." This is done using only natural ingredients, no artificial additives, slow fermentation – and baking with locally produced dairy products, eggs, and seasonal fruit.

The core of Amy's popularity is its incurably creative menu. The breads are infused with imported French and Greek olives, California walnuts and Texas pecans, and local herbs. The result is twenty different doughs every day, formed into a variety of uniquely flavored and textured loaves. Amy's pastry menu features berry, oatmeal, and cinnamon scones; muffins filled with seasonal fruit; chocolate cherry rolls, cinnamon raisin twists, applesauce doughnuts, cheese biscuits, butterscotch cashew bars, coconut cream cake, monkey cake, German chocolate cake, lemon mousseline cake; and at least ten varieties of cookies, including such exotica as kitchen sink, orange butter, lime cornmeal, white chocolate cherry chunker, and double chocolate pecan chubbie.

Oh, and did we mention that Amy's offers a great selection of sandwiches and salads? Let's face it, this store makes it irresistible to find out if man can live by Amy's Bread alone!

Address 672 Ninth Avenue (near 47th Street), New York 10036, Phone +1 212.977.2670, www.amysbread.com, info@amysbread.com | Transit Subway: 50 St (C, E); 42 St-Port Authority (A); 49 St (N, Q, R), Bus: M11, M20, M34, M42, M50, M104 | Hours Mon–Tue 7:30am–10pm, Wed–Fri 7:30am–11pm, Sat 8am–11pm, Sun 8am–10pm

5 Annie & Company Needlepoint and Knitting

They'll keep you in stitches

You start with a very, very long string. It may be thin and delicate or thick and strong. Through an elaborate orchestration of stitches, patterns, and colors, this long string eventually, magically, becomes a wearable garment or a decorative flourish on a worthy object. Because it is slowly and lovingly made by hand, the result is more cherished than a store-bought sweater or throw pillow.

Knitting is a practical skill, producing clothes for warmth, utility, and style – while needlepoint is a decorative art, adding embellishment to fabrics. Each takes dexterity, and both become *art* when imagination and creativity are woven in.

Annie & Company is the only store in Manhattan that caters extensively to both crafts under one roof. Annie opened her needlepoint shop in 2002 with the idea of having a warm and inviting environment – where people could not only buy everything needlepoint, but feel welcome to sit and stitch in an informal, friendly space. Later expanding it to include knitting as well, the supportive and expert staff made it a success. They'll happily help beginners get started, offering guidance, advice, and encouragement to customers through all phases of their projects. Classes and private lessons are also available for all skill levels.

Annie's has the largest selection of knitting and needlepoint supplies in NYC – printed and handpainted canvases and specialty threads for needlepoint; natural washable fibers and hand-dyed yarns for knitters; and an extensive library of patterns and designs for both. They can even customize designs if you want to get creative. And they offer all finishing services for both crafts.

There's a real sense of community in this comfortable, casual shop. Folks come to hang out, stitch or knit, and chat together at large tables or relax with their handiwork in comfortable club chairs. Come on in, you'll feel right at home.

Address 1763 Second Avenue (at 92nd Street), New York 10128, Phone +1 888.806.7200,
www.annieandco.com, annie@annieandco.com | Transit Subway: 96 St (6); 86 St (4, 5, 6),
Bus: M 15, M 31, M 86, M 96, M 102, M 103 | Hours Mon–Fri 11am–6pm, Sat
11am–5pm, Sun 12–5pm

6 Apple Store Grand Central
Sharing common ground

Steve Jobs was a genius at merging art and technology. Nowhere is this more apparent than on the east balcony of Grand Central Terminal, where you can tinker to your heart's delight with the latest Apple devices in a massive temple of architectural grandeur. But don't forget to lift your gaze from the iPads to the wondrous surroundings: celestial constellations on the restored zodiac ceiling, glittering gold-detailed chandeliers, the information booth's $20-million opal clock. From 1950–90 this balcony displayed Kodak's enormous 18x60-foot backlit color transparencies – a tourist attraction and technological marvel of its day. Today, both guided and audio tours are available to reveal the marvels and secrets of this historic building.

A century-old gem of Beaux-Arts architecture, the terminal now hosts Apple, *the* icon of technological innovation in the digital age. They share more common ground than just real estate. Grand Central is literally the gateway to America via networks of tracks crisscrossing the continent. And, with the invention of the iPhone, Apple became the virtual gateway to global connectivity. Both had rocky roads to success, and threats to their very existence. Thanks to Jackie Onassis' efforts to save Grand Central in the 1970s, it was spared demolition. And Apple's rollercoaster ride to success is by now legendary.

Overlooking the concourse where 750,000 people commute daily, you can hover above the fray in Apple's 23,000-square-foot marble-lined technology bubble – where they pay a million in annual rent and provide free wifi to the terminal. There are the usual long tables of enticing play-with-me products; workshop areas to educate and facilitate; two Genius Bars to unravel e-mysteries; and a retail area to buy new gadgetry. And for commuters shopping on the run, a quick pick-up line for purchases made from your seat on the train via – what else? – Apple's app.

Address 45 Grand Central Terminal (at Lexington Avenue), New York 10017, Phone +1 212.284.1800, www.apple.com/retail/grandcentral | Transit Subway: 42 St-Grand Central (4, 5, 6, 7, S), Bus: M 1, M 2, M 3, M 4, M 42, M 101, M 102, M 103 | Hours Mon–Fri 7am–9pm, Sat 10am–7pm, Sun 11am–6pm. Note: Apple Store at Fifth Avenue & 59th Street is open 24/7.

7 Argosy Book Store

Uncommon gifts for Everyman

Argosy proves that you don't have to be stuffy or elitist to be a world-class antiquarian bookshop. The quiet dignity of the store, the aroma of aging pages, the gold-stamped leather spines facing you as you stroll the aisles, all speak to the ivory tower image of such traditionally hallowed enterprises. But in fact Argosy's collections are eminently accessible – whether you're leafing through dollar books at the entrance or looking for a famous autograph worth thousands. The shop exudes the warm glow of cherished books and collectibles. The casually dressed bibliophiles working at their desks welcome your queries and enjoy the challenge of pinpointing your particular interests.

Founded in 1925, Argosy is now in its third generation of family ownership. All six floors of the turn-of-last-century building are stuffed with Americana, modern first editions, autographs, art, antique maps, prints, and histories of science, medicine, war, and peace.

When you come, allow plenty of time for leisurely browsing. After you've perused the major book collection on the main floor and basement, take the elevator to the second-floor Argosy Gallery specializing in vintage charts and maps, original prints, engravings, and woodcuts – all organized by subject. A must-see is the sixth-floor Autograph Room (which one of the owners refers to as 'the oh-my-god room'). Here you can find signatures and artifacts from the famous and infamous: American and international movie stars, presidents, scientists, sports figures, literary luminaries, theatrical headliners, politicians – notables from every walk of life.

The outdoor reduced-priced bins entice you to venture inside. The interior is laden with rarities, some of which are, admittedly, affordable only for the chosen few. Argosy's mission is "finding fantastic and unusual gifts for every fantastic and unusual person in your life." And maybe that person is you.

Address 116 East 59th Street (near Lexington Avenue), New York 10022, Phone +1 212.753.4455, www.argosybooks.com, argosy@argosybooks.com | Transit Subway: 59 St-Lexington Ave (4, 5, 6, N, Q, R); 63 St-Lexington Ave (F); Lexington Ave-53 St (E, M), Bus: M 1, M 2, M 3, M 4, M 31, M 57, M 101, M 102, M 103 | Hours Mon–Fri 10am–6pm, Sat 10am–5pm (except summer)

8 AsiaStore at Asia Society

Museum within a museum

In the great city of New York there may be hundreds of museums, ranging from world-class to wonky. Most have gift shops that add extra revenue to the cultural institution, and except for a few items particular to that museum, much of what you'll find is standard fare. But AsiaStore is a shining exception because what you find here is invariably exceptional.

From the moment you glide through the shop's undulating shoji-like screen wall from the lobby entrance, you're on a magical journey to the Far East. Explore. Admire lustrous silks and hand-dyed fabrics of ingeniously styled garments, bags, and accessories; luminous hand-blown vases that rival the beauty of the flowers they hold; one-of-a-kind jewelry crafted from surprising materials and unusual stones; textiles, stationery, and prints based on the museum's own art; and innovative renditions of classic housewares. Find yourself enveloped in a dreamlike experience of pattern, texture, and color, as exotic music and scents waft through the shop. Peruse the extensive book section with titles on Asian art, culture, cooking, literature, and philosophy.

The mission of Asia Society – which hosts both the museum and its shop – is to bring traditional and contemporary Asian and Asian-American art to an ever-broader audience. The store prides itself on presenting the best in Asian design and literature. It features the renowned brands of Asia and showcases exciting new work of talented designers and artisans in varied media, many shown exclusively at Asia Society. Every purchase encourages and supports emerging artists and creative expression.

AsiaStore is in itself a curated collection, acquired by scouring Asian marketplaces in search of distinctive designs, traditional handicrafts, and vintage treasures. *Zagat's 2013 New York City Shopping Guide* insightfully calls it a "little museum inside the museum."

Address 725 Park Avenue (at 70th Street), New York 10021, Phone +1 212.327.9217,
www.asiastore.org, asiastore@asiasociety.org | Transit Subway: 68 St-Hunter College (6),
63 St-Lexington Ave (F), Bus: M 1, M 2, M 3, M 4, M 15, M 66, M 72, M 101, M 102,
M 103 | Hours Mon–Sun 11am–6pm, Fri 11am–9pm

9 Beads of Paradise

The magic of adornment

You're irresistibly attracted to this brilliantly colorful shop simply because of its exuberance. Sitting on a side street just steps from Union Square, the store is known for its constantly changing radiant window displays. Wander inside and the effect is amplified by a bewildering array of beads, artifacts and relics from around the world. The shop is like a wrapped gift, a brightly decorated, dazzling package. You're drawn in by an Afro-beat or the strains of remixed Hindustani music, and a warm greeting.

A friendly staff of talented artisans, who create much of the shop's distinctive jewelry, can lead you through the endless assortment of ornaments. Design your own unique piece from a vast collection of beads in wood, shell, metal, glass, amber, semi-precious stones, gold, silver. Choose from antique European trade glass, contemporary West African powder glass, wooden Nepalese prayer beads, exquisite Australian opals. If you're a beginner, join their weekend class to get started. Advanced workshops are also offered for higher skill levels.

As prominent as the jewelry is an astounding collection of art and curios from many exotic cultures. The owners travel the world in search of the exceptional – hand-woven Thai silk scarves, Native American tribal art, ancient African funerary ceramics. Each piece is imbued with some sort of significance, harkening back to a time before mass-production. Themed displays reveal an understanding of the cultures they portray – Afghan nomadic jewelry or the wall of Mexican Day-of-the-Dead relics.

But this intense shop is still primarily about the beads and their eternal significance of ritual and ornament to humankind. From basic elements and tools for jewelry-making to millennia-old glass beads from China, a visit to Beads of Paradise can truly transport you to a place where, dare we say, the magic of self-adornment is still alive and well.

Address 16 East 17th Street (near Fifth Avenue), New York 10003, Phone +1 212.620.0642, www.beadsofparadisenyc.com, info@beadsofparadisenyc.com | Transit Subway: Union Sq–14 St (N, Q, R, L, 4, 5, 6); 14 St (F), Bus: M1, M3, M5, M7, M14 | Hours Mon–Sat 11am–7:30pm, Sun 12–6:30pm

10_Bellydance America

Bedazzled by the beauty

The bling therapy alone is worth a visit to this exotic fashion emporium – a glimmering contrast to New York's *urban chic* fashion palette of black and grey. Stepping inside, you're transported to the marketplace of a foreign land with hypnotic music and bursts of color from glittering, crafted wares. The hand-carved shelves are laden with ornate treasures and a hundred drums lined up in formation. Moroccan, Bedouin, and Egyptian goods hang from the ceiling and decorate the walls. Find elaborate costumes, crocheted, beaded and coin scarves, amulets, genie lamps, jewelry, musical instruments, dancing swords, original paintings, vintage and antique tapestries. Ancient and modern are displayed side-by-side, trendy styles alongside classic favorites. Alluring bra-and-belt sets, spangled headwear, semi-precious tribal jewelry, *haute couture* and custom-designed outfits all tempt you to become the seductress hidden inside you.

Bellydance America is a mecca for lovers of Middle Eastern, North African, and South Asian fashion, music, and dance. Husband-wife owners Hanna and Jehan entertain you with captivating tales and happily give impromptu demonstrations of their art. The passion is infectious.

This magical boutique was the first – and still the only – bellydance supply shop in the city. In a second-floor suite in the heart of the Fashion District, BDA has spacious performance studios for dance and music that attract artists and celebrities from all over the world. Middle Eastern bands and orchestras rehearse here, too, so you may be treated to a free concert if you show up at the right time. Lessons are also offered in salsa, kizomba, burlesque, hip-hop, ballet, jazz, and drumming. Top international instructors teach the art of bellydancing. Once enticed, check their website to find and enjoy a bellydance performance at a local club or nearby venue. Prepare to be dazzled.

Address 265 West 37th Street (near Eighth Avenue), Suite 203, New York 10018, Phone +1 212.768.4888, www.bellydanceamerica.com | Transit Subway: 34 St-Penn Sta (A, C, E); 42 St-Times Sq (1, 2, 3, 7, N, Q, R), Bus: M7, M20, M34 | Hours Tue–Sun 11am–7pm

11__C.O. Bigelow

America's oldest apothecary

For centuries apothecaries have been the locus of healing treatments prepared by experts. Founded by a doctor in 1838, C.O. Bigelow is the oldest one in the country. For over 175 years it has been a pioneer in personal care products, health and beauty aids. To this day, at its original Greenwich Village site, the store still honors the tradition of custom-made remedies.

Even with the invasion of cut-rate chain drugstores within a few blocks in every direction, Bigelow remains a neighborhood mainstay. More than a pharmacy, it is a place of discovery, conversation, learning, and community. They carry a wide range of international and hard-to-find cosmetics, organic beauty supplies, and homeopathic remedies. Many products are named for the doctor-practitioners who created them. Each tells a different story of its apothecary heritage. Their organic skincare products combine centuries-old preparations with modern ingredients sourced from around the world.

Over the years, Bigelow has serviced some of America's most prominent figures, including Eleanor Roosevelt, Mark Twain, and Thomas Edison. The store still attracts an A-list of celebrity clientele, like Susan Sarandon, Calvin Klein, and Sarah Jessica Parker. And their own brand of affordable beauty products made from historic recipes exploiting the power of natural ingredients attracts a loyal following. The Apothecary's Rose, for example, contains essential oils and effective nutrients to nourish healthy skin, and used to be advertised as a remedy for indigestion, sore throats, skin rashes, and eye maladies.

A knowledgeable, attentive staff takes pride in its reputation as *Honest, Genuine, Trustworthy* – a motto painted boldly on tall pillars in their elegant, chandeliered salon-like store. As one patron described this New York institution, it's a shopping experience "laced with history instead of buttertop frosting."

Address 414 Sixth Avenue (near 9th Street), New York 10011, Phone +1 212.533.2700, www.cobigelow.com, customerservice@cobigelow.com | Transit Subway: West 4 St (A, B, C, D, E, F, M); Christopher St-Sheridan Sq (1, 2); 14 St-6 Ave (1, 2, 3, F, L, M), Bus: M 1, M 2, M 3, M 5, M 7, M 8, M 14, M 20 | Hours Mon–Fri 7:30am–9pm, Sat 8:30am–7pm, Sun 8:30am–5:30pm

12   Blatt Billiards
A player's paradise

A stroll to the back of this spacious showroom reveals a whole section with improbable stacks of elaborately carved and decorated billiard tables, piled so high they barely dodge the beautiful poolroom light fixtures hanging from the ceiling. Their new space, relocated from the original downtown showroom/factory, displays over sixty antique and customcrafted tables of various period and contemporary designs, handcrafted to perfection with inlays, carvings, and trims. Reproductions of vintage models are hard to distinguish from the originals, though they sell for about one-third the price. To create these high-ticket replicas (starting at $25 K) Blatt's skilled craftsmen build each table individually – shaping wood, fitting joints, hand-polishing corners, cutting slate tops, and finally assembling at the customer's site. Among their clientele are the very wealthy and famous, those who demand the very best.

This company began in the roaring twenties, when money and speakeasy booze flowed freely, and the city boasted a few thousand pool halls. Samuel Blatt started hand-crafting pool cues and billiard balls, then repairing and servicing tables for these lucrative establishments. In the lean years of the Great Depression, Blatt helped his customers survive by extending credit and affordably restoring worn tables. But during WWII, as America's young men went off to war, pool halls largely disappeared, leaving Blatt to buy up equipment from the many defunct businesses. Ultimately, he acquired the world's largest collection of antique billiard tables.

All the accessories are here, from cue tips to padded spectator seats. Dozens of sparkling dart sets remind us that there's more to Blatt than billiards: also chess, backgammon, shuffleboard, air-hockey, foosball. The consummate gamester will feel right at home here – where the air is infused with the excitement of keen competition.

Address 330 West 38th Street (near Eighth Avenue), New York 10018, Phone +1 212.674.8855, www.blattbilliards.com, info@blattbilliards.com | Transit Subway: 42 St-Port Authority (A, C, E); 42 St-Times Sq (1, 2, 3, 7, N, Q, R), Bus: M 7, M 11, M 20, M 34, M 42, M 104 | Hours Mon–Fri 9am–6:30pm, Sat 10am–5pm

13 Bluestockings Books

Just your friendly anarchist bookstore

In days of yore, a feisty group of progressive British women were known as "Bluestockings," a term later applied to upstart ladies with radical agendas, like equal rights. Aptly named for what began as a feminist bookstore in New York in 1999, Bluestockings became the premier radical bookshop and activist cafe located on the Lower East Side – not coincidentally the birthplace of the American punk rock movement.

Now run as a collectively-owned bookstore with a conscience, it stocks works to inform, illuminate, stimulate, and provoke readers all across the political spectrum. From Abu-Jamal to Zizek they carry fiction, non-fiction, brave memoirs, niche erotica, independent 'zines, pamphlets, and periodicals you won't find elsewhere in the city. But there's much more to this homey haven on Allen Street. From their altruistic mission statement you can glean its social value: "Bluestockings is a radical bookstore, fair trade cafe, and activist center. Through words, art, food, activism, education, and community, we strive to create a space that welcomes and empowers all people. We actively support movements that challenge hierarchy and all systems of oppression… to make our space and resources available to such movements for meetings, events, and research… and offer educational programming that promotes centered, strategic, and visionary thinking, towards the realization of a society that is infinitely creative, truly democratic, equitable, ecological, and free."

Bluestockings hosts progressive cultural events – provocative talks, panel discussions, movie premieres, and open-mike nights, attracting luminaries like the incendiary Russian rock band Pussy Riot, journalist Amy Goodman of *Democracy Now*, and anthropologist/anarchist author David Graeber. Come in for a hot cuppa joe or an herbal tea, read your morning paper or political manifesto at a quiet window table, and watch the world go by.

Address 172 Allen Street (near Rivington Street), New York 10002, Phone +1 212.777.6028, www.bluestockings.com, info@bluestockings.com | Transit Subway: 2nd Ave (F), Bus: B 39, M 9, M 14A, M 15, M 21 | Hours Daily 11am –11pm

14 Books of Wonder

Where Mother Goose meets Harry Potter

Babar and Curious George usher you through the revolving doors, and you're instantly transported back in time to your own childhood, even if you're leading an eager youngster by the hand.

All your favorite book friends live in this cavernous reading room, happy to see you again. Old acquaintances are renewed, new adventures begin. If you come in with a child – or to buy for one – just about every new title and old classic can be found on these shelves. The atmosphere is welcoming, cheery, unhurried. Kids sit cross-legged in the wide aisles, turning pages, surrounded by piles of books.

Books of Wonder's original tiny Greenwich Village shop was actually the model for the movie *You've Got Mail*, where owner Meg Ryan is threatened by a big chain store putting her out of business – a Samson-and-Goliath parable for today's retail environment. But what has kept BOW alive and well (while many chains have failed) is its personal attention, depth of knowledge, and love of the subject that can't be matched by mega-stores. The shop's actual owner, Peter Glassman, has made the bookstore a community-minded gathering place for locals and visitors alike, hosting weekly storytimes, book signings with authors and illustrators, and community events to attract all age groups. A friendly snack bar gives parents and kids a relaxing place to nibble while they read.

From the classics to the latest, no bookstore in the city has a more complete children's selection. Spend some time browsing the gallery, with original framed artworks from vintage to contemporary books, and the impressive library of antique and rare books. Committed to preserving the best of the genre, Books of Wonder re-issued all fourteen OZ books with their original illustrations and published over sixty classic children's titles under its own imprint.

Like walking through the secret door in Narnia, we've somehow landed in a magical world.

Address 18 West 18th Street (near Fifth Avenue), New York 10011, Phone +1 212.989.3270, www.booksofwonder.com, info@booksofwonder.com | **Transit** Subway: 18 St (1, 2); 14 St (F, M); 14 St-Union Sq (4, 5, 6, L, N, Q, R), Bus: M1, M2, M3, M5, M7, M14, M20, M23 | **Hours** Mon–Sat 10am–7pm, Sun 11am–6pm

15_Bowne & Co. Stationers

Making a good impression

You can almost hear the drum go rat-a-tat and the fife tootle out the strains of *Yankee Doodle*. You're transported back in time to the American Revolution. New York was emerging as an economic epicenter of the Colonies and new businesses were sprouting up everywhere. Established in 1775, Bowne & Co is one of city's oldest and longest-running businesses – and still a working press – with a gift shop drawing visitors from all over. Its location on Water Street, part of South Street Seaport Museum, replicates a traditional printing and stationer's shop offering an authentic early American experience.

Nearly 250 years ago, the original store, founded by merchant and philanthropist Robert Bowne, sold dry goods. Owing to its proximity to banks and investment firms on Wall Street, Bowne later focused on stationery and printing, specializing in financial documents. Original inventory lists show gilt-edge writing paper, straw paper, ledger books, and seamen's journals. Today, the print shop recalls an era when everything was done by hand. There is still handset wood and metal movable type, and seven historic hand-operated letterpresses. Skilled pressmen crank up nineteenth-century equipment to carry on a tradition of small-job printing for clients who value authenticity and handcrafted work. Bowne & Co's artist and master printer Robert Warner is on site to share his expertise.

The charm of Bowne's atmospheric gift shop lures you with its selection of creative souvenirs produced on their antiquated presses. Impress someone, bring home a sample: *Map of Lower Manhattan Circa 1835 Broadside;* or a set of six *Style Coasters* illustrating the characters of a classic typeface; or *Rebus*, a printed adventure story told with pictures interspersed with words; or assorted postcard sets, like *Flying V* birds, and *Frogz on Bikez*. One thing is certain: whatever you take away will be hot off the press!

Address 209–211 Water Street (near Fulton Street), New York 10038, Phone
+1 646.315.4478, www.southstreetseaportmuseum.org, bowneprinters@seany.org |
Transit Subway: Fulton St (2, 3, 4, 5, A, C, J); City Hall (R), Bus: M 9, M 15, M 22, M 103 |
Hours Daily 11am–7pm

16_ Brooklyn Botanic Garden Shop

A lot more than just a walk in the park

You know what they say: *location, location, location!* One of the many reasons to visit this bright, spacious plant emporium is exactly that. It sits on the perimeter of the lush 52-acre Brooklyn Botanic Garden, across the street from the world-class Brooklyn Museum, and a short walk from Prospect Park and its charming zoo. A day spent exploring this neighborhood offers an opportunity to experience a country setting in all its pastoral glory with a healthy serving of fine art and culture in the mix. In Brooklyn!

The official gift shop of Brooklyn Botanic Garden aims to delight, inspire, and educate. This airy, light-infused shop is a pleasure to browse, with its great variety of plant-centric items. You'll surely find something to bring home, whether for your apartment's windowsill or your great estate's front lawn – perhaps a sculptural bonsai, a quirky cactus, an exotic orchid, or a succulent tropical. There are potted greens for indoors and colorful seasonals for outdoors. An extensive selection of seeds and bulbs appeals to gardening buffs of all stripes, from veggie-growers to specialty hobbyists. Their diverse collection of thriving terrariums, both tabletops and hanging globes, tempts even those who don't have a green thumb.

But there's more here than denizens of the plant kingdom – flowerpots and decorative pottery, smart garden tools, housewares, an impressive book section to guide, inform, and entertain, as well as garden-inspired artisanal jewelry and clothing, plant-based bath and beauty products, and nature-oriented games and toys. And you can find something affordable for every budget.

When you exit the shop, stop for a bite to eat at the Terrace Cafe down the path. And as you wander through the lovingly tended grounds of the Botanic Garden you'll grow to appreciate one of the most splendid treasures of New York – Brooklyn's great outdoors!

Address 990 Washington Avenue (near Classon Avenue), Brooklyn 11225, Phone +1 718.622.0963, http://shop.bbg.org, shop@bbg.org | Transit Subway: Eastern Pkwy-Brooklyn Museum (2, 3); Prospect Park (B, Q, S); Franklin Ave (4, 5), Bus: B 48, B 45 | Hours Tue – Sun 10am – 6pm

17 Brooklyn Ice Cream Factory

Fire and ice (cream)

Approaching from a distance by land or by water you see a narrow wooden building with a brooding watchtower rising high in the air above the old Fulton Ferry Landing. This retired 1920s fireboat house was converted in 2001 and became one of Brooklyn's favorite ice cream parlors. Its spectacular location offers a unique view of New York: a sweeping panorama highlighted by the proud Statue of Liberty in the harbor, the majestic Manhattan skyline, and the famed Brooklyn Bridge, so close you can almost touch it.

The store was opened shortly after 9/11 by owner and ice cream specialist Mark Thompson, who produces his tasty treats small batches at a time – eight flavors in all – with no added preservatives. The *New York Times* rhapsodized that the frozen treats are "creamy, ethereally light and perfectly balanced. They practically float into your mouth." The homemade taste of pure and simple ice cream wins the day. (Not to mention the generous portions!) The toppings, syrups, and other all-natural ingredients are of the highest quality – whether you favor cones, sundaes, milk shakes, banana splits or any other of their imaginative creamy concoctions. The texture is old-fashioned and slightly grainy, with sweetness kept to a palate-teasing minimum. This ice cream bears no relation to the mass-produced variety churned out in the factory vats of big-brand companies.

Long lines of patiently-waiting local patrons and visiting tourists, flanked by impatient children frolicking about, spill out of the Factory's front doors and reach across the plaza area, where people flock to take in the dramatic view and hear the distant strains of the nearby carousel.

Of course, you can get to the Ice Cream Factory by public transit, including the East River Ferry which disembarks practically at its door. But who can resist the temptation – weather permitting – to walk across the historic Brooklyn Bridge!

Address 1 Water Street (near Old Fulton Street), Brooklyn 11201, Phone +1 718.246.3963, www.brooklynicecreamfactory.com | Transit Subway: High St (A, C); York St (F); Clark St (2, 3), Bus: B 25 | Hours Daily 12–10pm

18__ The Brooklyn Kitchen & The Meathook

A blissful marriage

These two unique entities are far more than a grocer and a butcher sharing the same space – they are the successful union of two food services united by their love of quality, education, and high consciousness. Together they constitute a complete *cooking store* devoted to making their customers comfortable in the kitchen and with their ingredients. They carry every conceivably useful cooking utensil and tool; offer technique-based classes; sell fresh produce, quality flours and spices, and locally made and packaged foods; and are a first-class butcher shop – all to ensure that you have a good time cooking and that you're eating real food.

Inspiration for The Brooklyn Kitchen came in 2006 to owners Taylor and Harry when it was time to harvest the grapes in their Williamsburg backyard. Nowhere in the neighborhood could they find jars or pectin to preserve jelly and jams. Figuring that other budding local epicures would need a place to buy their first good knife, the idea for The Brooklyn Kitchen was conceived.

Initially, they just sold cooking tools and books. When they started offering pig-butchering instruction – where a dozen people looked on as a pig became pork chops – the small, intimate classes sold out immediately. Clearly there was a niche market of serious food devotees.

Nearby, a dedicated group of young butchers founded The Meat Hook, a custom-cut butchery specializing in grass-fed local beef and specialty sausages. They help customers understand that many lesser-known cuts may provide better flavor and a more interesting cooking experience.

When The Meat Hook joined up with The Brooklyn Kitchen in one location, a rare bonding emerged, forming a happy, healthy family born of the fortuitous union of taste and caring.

Address 100 Frost Street (near Leonard Street), Brooklyn 11211, Phone +1 718.389.2982, www.thebrooklynkitchen.com, info@thebrooklynkitchen.com | Transit Subway: Metropolitan Ave (G); Lorimer St (L), Bus: B 24, B 43, B 48, B 62, Q 59 | Hours Mon–Sat 10am–8pm, Sun 12–6pm

19___Casa de las Velas

Let there be light

The traditional *botanica* is a shop that sells candles, charms, herbs, and other religious ritual and spiritual items, especially those associated with Santería – a religion of West African and Caribbean origin that fuses Roman Catholicism with other ancient and esoteric beliefs. The aim of the botanica is to help needy souls who suffer with personal or spiritual problems: from asthma to love-life to lawsuits to depression. Casa de las Velas (House of Candles) is the city's oldest existing botanica, originating in 1921 and dispensing curative offerings to its local multi-cultural community to the present day – where it not only sells a wide variety of spiritual *objets*, but offers religious consultations, often accompanied by customized blessings to make your purchases more potent.

Candles may be the first lure of this colorful and odiferous emporium, but the diverse religious heritage is clearly projected through the grimacing deities hanging from the ceiling; shelves lined with a multitude of figurines of Catholic saints mingled with pagan deities; and a mixture of traditional church artifacts with popular folk remedies. At the back is an extensive assortment of fresh and dried herbs that may be prescribed for all sorts of ailments, along with incense, talismans, sculptured candles, bath salts, and even floor wash to help bless your home. Many additional cures may recommend the use of honeys, oils, perfumes, powders, spices, and minerals. An impressive collection of religious books in both English and Spanish can offer further guidance.

Casa de las Velas, above all, may be seen as a spiritual center for esoteric Afro-Caribbean traditions – Santería, but also Espiritismo, Palo Mayombe, and others dealing with both good and evil spirits, and sometimes black magic. Evil may be dispelled with enlightenment. And enlightenment can at times be reached through a simple scented candle.

Address 60 East 116th Street (near Madison Avenue), New York 10029, **Phone** +1 212.722.4999, rosamaria1029@gmail.com | **Transit** Subway: 116 St (6), Bus: M 1, M 102, M 103, M 116 | **Hours** Mon–Sat 10am–6pm, Sun 12–6pm

B Ordoñez

20__Casey Rubber Stamps

Ye olde stamping ground

You may not be in the market for a rubber stamp, but you don't want to miss this one-of-a-kind mini-factory. Or the opportunity to chat with the inimitable John Casey, who has been handcrafting rubber stamps since the early eighties. With his twinkly wit and snappy Irish brogue, Casey is a pleasure to engage, discussing art, science, the weather, or, yes, his vast collection. Shelves loaded with baskets and boxes of old stamps and new are sorted by theme, others tossed in a stew of unrelated images.

This lilliputian shop is magical. Indeed, the cramped space is part of the charm; walls lined floor to ceiling with 3-dimensional woodblocks to press out 2-dimensional graphics. The digital jpeg-to-rubber-stamp technology can create custom stamps from virtually any supplied image. That constitutes about half his business; the other half is selling pre-fabricated stamps for as little as $3.

The shop is an eye-popping repository of deftly sorted piles of rubber stamps – a visual potpourri of quirky *Alice in Wonderland* characters, ravens, frogs, octopi, hot-air balloons, spider webs, teeth, Manhattan skyline, patriotic themes, and even a life-size bedbug!

While most of his stamp production is geared for graphic designers, local artists, and fashionistas, much of his customizing business appeals to stray shoppers who happen to meander past this hole-in-the-wall storefront deep in the East Village. They'll discover a chance to create innovative party invitations or whimsical stationery. Children are some of his best clients, for obvious reasons.

Taking a unique, if cavalier, approach to business, his official hours and policy are posted on the door: "Open when not closed. Closed when not open. We are child, dog & eccentric friendly." With characteristic humor Casey quips, "What I want written on my tombstone is, *He made a good impression.*"

Address 322 East 11th Street (near Second Avenue), New York 10003, Phone
+1 917.669.4151, www.caseyrubberstamps.com | Transit Subway: 1st Ave-14 St (L); Astor
Pl (6), Bus: M 8, M 15, M 14, M 102, M 103 | Hours Mon–Tue 2–8pm, Wed–Sat 1–8pm

21 Chelsea Market

A cavernous foodland

If you don't mind the human conveyor belt of shoppers and browsers ambling through its serpentine passageways, you'll find Chelsea Market – New York's trendiest culinary attraction – to be an international food orgy! For tourists and local foodies alike, the forty-odd ethnic and artisanal eateries and shops dazzle the eyes, tweak the nose, and seduce the palate. (Some non-food entities happily coexist here: barber, bookshop, boutiques, newsstand – but the focus is definitely on *eating*.)

Exploring this subterranean-esque bazaar you'll discover food, drink, and accouterments from virtually every corner of the epicurean world. It's all here – literally soup to nuts, pate to gelato. A partial list: breads, crepes, sushi, spices, tacos, wine, spirits, meats, seafood, pastries, herbs, cheeses, fresh produce, teas, coffees, and gourmet and health foods. Eat your way through, or buy to take home and cook.

Occupying the footprint of a full city block in the hyper-hip Meatpacking District, Chelsea Market shares the building with hi-tech companies like You Tube and Google. So the mingling crowd is as cool as it gets.

Possibly most outstanding, however, is the environment itself. Originally a biscuit factory (where the Oreo cookie was invented!), the decor is 'reclaimed post-industrial' – shop-lined tunnels with stripped-down brick walls and archways, polished concrete floors, exposed ducts and pipes, giant factory fans, sanded steel doors, corrugated ceilings, raw I-beams, stone benches, salvaged architectural artifacts, works of art, and at its center, a deep well fed by a gushing overhead drainpipe psychedelically morphing colors. This *Brave New World* environment is undeniably cheerful, with a built-in sense of humor. Everyone smiles. It must be experienced in all its incongruity to be appreciated. So when you visit, don't just bring a big appetite – bring your sense of adventure as well!

Address 75 Ninth Avenue (at 15th Street), New York 10011, Phone +1 212.652.2110, www.chelseamarket.com, michael@chelseamarket.com | Transit Subway: 14 St (A, C, E); 8th Ave (L); 14 St (1, 2, 3), Bus: M11, M14, M20 | Hours Mon–Sat 7am–9pm, Sun 8am–8pm

22__Chess Forum

A place to check with a mate

It's one of those camouflaged shops you could walk right past and not even notice, unless you're setting out to find it. It blends with the old tenement buildings on a charming Greenwich Village street and looks like a lot less than what it actually has to offer.

Chess Forum is the last of the old-time dedicated stores in a neighborhood once known as Manhattan's chess district. Just a few blocks south of the world-famous Marshall Chess Club (where 13-year-old Bobby Fischer won "the game of the century") and the famous public chess tables of Washington Square Park – this heady shop attracts chess buffs looking for a game, a new set, or just the companionship of fellow chess geeks.

It was in that spirit that Chess Forum was founded in 1995, to create an environment where chess-minded people could meet and exchange thoughts and ideas. In the clubby atmosphere, players can relax over a game while sipping tea, coffee, or soft drinks. You can even bring your own bottle of wine.

The range of clientele is impressive – from toddlers to seniors, beginners to grandmasters, students to professors, artists, scientists, soldiers, policemen, ex-cons, and celebrities. The forward-thinking Chess Forum provides lessons and weekend classes for children, and even a summer camp program.

The retail section of the shop offers a wide selection of chess and backgammon sets, along with other board games like checkers, Go, dominoes, cribbage, and mah-jongg. Chess Forum also has a fine library of chess books for browsing and purchase.

Owner Imad Khachan recalls a favorite moment: Some years ago, rock superstar David Lee Roth came in regularly for chess lessons. Once, a customer recognized him and asked if he was really Diamond Dave. He responded, "In here I'm just another guy and my name is David. But outside, and once I put on those sunglasses, I become Diamond Dave and you cannot talk to me."

Address 219 Thompson Street (near Bleecker), New York 10012, Phone +1 212.475.2369, www.chessforum.com, info@chessforum.com | **Transit** Subway: West 4 St (A, B, C, D, E, F, M); Houston St (1, 2, 3), Bus: M 5, M 21 | **Hours** Daily 11am–midnight

23 CityStore

NYC's official souvenir shop

Where do you go if you want to take home a *real* piece of NYC – like a genuine horseshoe worn by the mighty steeds of the city's mounted police? CityStore! In the lobby of the landmark Municipal Building in Manhattan's Civic Center near the Brooklyn Bridge walkway, this shop is a hidden trove for visitors and city-dwellers alike. Owned and operated by the city government, all sales go directly into its coffers. The cheerful, vividly colorful shop is loaded with NYC-themed mementos, many of which can only be purchased here.

Opened in 1981 as a small, rather dull, municipal outlet, City Books sold the official City Directory, obscure government publications, and a few souvenirs. Recognizing its potential for retail success, it was later expanded, renamed CityStore, and transformed into a full-fledged souvenir-hunter's utopia, with licensed merchandise from various city departments: Police, Fire, Sanitation, Parks, and Subway. There's a wide array of goodies, from the usual hats, t-shirts and magnets, to fine silk scarves, babywear, toys, 3-D puzzles, and books about the Big Apple.

Some of the best finds are quirky, fun, and unexpected. Authentic park signage *(Central Park; Battery Park; No people except in the company of a dog)*, vintage taxi medallions, manhole cover trivets, subway token cufflinks, tenement radiator lapel pins. CityStore's annex, a block away and right inside the Marriage Bureau, is a florist shop – no wedding is complete without flowers – plus favors announcing with typical bravura: *I Got Married in NYC*. Rhinestone-embedded Bride & Groom baseball caps have a white veil on the bride's hat, of course.

Find memorabilia for everyone on your list, including yourself. The landmark building is an esthetic treat for anyone with an eye for traditional architecture. Step back and admire the majestic facade. Gracing its top is a dynamic statue, aptly named *Civic Fame*.

Address 1 Centre Street, North Plaza (near Chambers Street), New York 10007, Phone +1 212.639.9675, www.nyc.gov/citystore, citystore@dcas.nyc.gov | Transit Subway: Brooklyn Bridge (4, 5, 6); Chambers St (J); City Hall (R), Bus: M 9, M 22, M 103 | Hours Mon–Fri 10am–5pm

24 Deco Jewels

All that glitters is not gold

"If a bit of sparkle can light up my face, then a lot of sparkle can light up a room!" That thought put Janice Berkson on a path to becoming an obsessive collector of the dazzling vintage gems and Lucite handbags that fill her Soho shop. The tidy little store glitters with costume jewelry dating from the roaring twenties to the psychedelic sixties – necklaces, bracelets, pins, clip-on earrings, and a formidable collection of cuff links from kitschy to classy. And that stunning array of 1950s purses!

She always loved shopping and dressing up. Bargain-hunting at flea markets and thrift shops, she got hooked by so many glitzy baubles, she decided to sell some off. That was 1982 – no eBay or Etsy yet – so she rented a table at an uptown street fair and made a quick $300. She saw the potential for a retail business at a time when superstars Madonna and Cyndi Lauper were strutting vintage glamour and rhinestone bling. Berkson took space in Soho, a popular area of artists and galleries that attracted shoppers and tourists. When she discovered vintage Lucite handbags, she added them to her line and became a collector, eventually writing a coffee-table book on the subject, *Carry Me! 1950s Lucite Bags*. Berkson was attracted to these mid-century fashion novelties as "functional objects of art, architectural sculptures."

America's post-WWII optimism, originality, and affluence spawned creativity and consumerism. It showed up in fashion, and women loved to flaunt the latest flamboyant styles. Costume jewelry flourished. Hard plastic purses of Lucite came in all different shapes and colors and some were wondrous feats of engineering, containing sliding compartments, and matching sets of compacts, lighters, and cigarette cases.

These glitzy *objets* now fill Deco Jewels. Berkson's passion for vintage bling is contagious. Spend a few minutes chatting with her and you'll come away feeling sparkly yourself.

Address 131 Thompson Street (near Prince Street), New York 10012, Phone +1 212.253.1222, decojewels@earthlink.net | Transit Subway: Spring St (C, E); Prince St (N, R); Houston St (1); Broadway-Lafayette (B, D, F, M), Bus: M 5, M 20, M 21 | Hours Daily 12–7pm

25__ The Demolition Depot
An almost-museum of artifacts

Along Harlem's main thoroughfare you'll find something quite unexpected: an old warehouse loaded with architectural treasures. Demolition Depot has collected and sorted parts of buildings for over forty years. Salvaging projects have included the Commodore, Biltmore, and Vanderbilt hotels, Audubon Ballroom, Helen Hayes Theater, and New York Life Building. When a historic structure comes down, Demolition Depot mines it for collectibles with stories to tell: John D. Rockefeller Jr's fireplace mantel; Oscar Hammerstein's office chandelier; Pierre Cardin's Art Deco bar from Maxim's restaurant. Artifacts range from 1600s medieval to 1960s mid-century modern, and all periods in between.

The backyard garden is an eerie wonderland of terracotta dragons and angels, stone gargoyles, marble urns, clocks frozen in time, ironwork, keystones, gas lamps, and mystery items of unknown purpose. The main floor houses lighting from gothic candelabras to gaudy chandeliers, display cases from functional to fantastical, and hardware defying identification. As you wind your way up the dusty wooden staircase, surprises crowd every landing. The next floor is aglow with framed stained and leaded glass and antique furniture. Upstairs is a veritable forest of doors and mantelpieces. The top floor overflows with vintage plumbing, ovens, medicine cabinets, mirrors – ordinary to exquisite, and dozens of old bicycles suspended from the tin ceiling.

Owner Evan Blum knows his stuff. He appraises for Sotheby's and Christie's and consults on period decor with interior designers of high-end hotels and residences. Want to replicate a certain period or own a bit of architectural history? They can ship it, no matter its size or destination. Recently a vintage bar went to Germany, light fixtures to Hong Kong, bathroom fittings to Tasmania. Or just browse the multitude of museum-worthy *objets* – but here you're allowed to touch.

Address 216 East 125th Street (near Second Avenue), New York 10035, Phone
+1 212.860.1138, www.demolitiondepot.com, info@demolitiondepot.com | Transit
Subway: 125 St (4, 5, 6), Bus: M 1, M 15, M 35, M 60, M 100, M 101, M 103 | Hours
Mon–Fri 10am–6pm, Sat 11am–6pm

26 — Doodle Doo's

Cutting-edge fun with star trimmings

Gone are the days when a parent had to coax a crying child into a barber's chair for that first haircut. Kids enthusiastically scramble through the doors of colorful Doodle Doo's to climb aboard one of the cool kiddie-ride seats and be pampered by an expert stylist savvy in the ways of cajoling small children. This salon, toy store, boutique, and party hotspot is all wrapped up in one energetic, whimsical universe. It also offers mini-manicures, updo's, ear-piercing, or a simple bangs trim.

Boys and girls love the haircut stations, each equipped with a mini-chair in the shape of a boat, taxi or car, and — to hold their attention — a monitor playing favorite videos. Free lollipops and bubbles are the reward with every cut, keeping the experience as pain-free as possible for both youngsters and adults. A congratulatory first haircut comes with a certificate, a gift bag, and a lock of hair for posterity!

Owner Dana Rywelski, the busy mother of two, is, in today's vernacular, a true *momtrepreneur*. This former nanny with a masters in early childhood education knows all about the struggle to get a child's hair cut — so combining a fun salon experience with the enticement of toy and clothes shopping, makes it a win-win for both parent and child. Dana reasons that when kids are happy and occupied, parents relax and can browse the eco-friendly selection of clothes, games, books, hair accessories, and imaginative gifts that fill this bubbly wonderland.

A downstairs space accommodates birthday parties and special occasions. While girls usually favor glitter-drenched glamour hairstyling, boys go for face-painting, wash-off tattoos, and hair-sculpting. Don't be surprised to see a familiar face or two here. Doodle Doo's is a favorite among neighborhood celeb parents like Liv Tyler, Amy Poehler, Sarah Jessica Parker, and Kate Winslet. So much fun going on here, and that's just trimming the edges!

Address 11 Christopher Street (near Greenwich Avenue), New York 10014, Phone +1 212.627.3667, www.doodledoos.com, doodle@doodledoos.com | Transit Subway: Christopher St-Sheridan Sq (1); West 4 St (A, B, C, D, E, F, M); 14 St (2, 3), Bus: M 1, M 2, M 3, M 5, M 7, M 8, M 14, M 20 | Hours Mon – Sat 10am – 6pm, Sun 11am – 5pm

27 Drama Book Shop
A mecca for performing artists

With so many independent bookstores falling by the wayside, it's a good sign that there's still a demand for specialty shops with savvy staffs of working professionals. Drama Book Shop epitomizes this phenomenon. Everything in print relating to show business – theater, film, TV – is here, plus a multifarious selection of multimedia materials to help the aspiring thespian nail down a dialect or strike that classic pose.

Near Times Square, the jazzy epicenter of Broadway theater, DBS is unquestionably the city's best source for theatrical works, with 8,000 scripts (in various languages), plus songbooks, biographies, theater and trade periodicals, and how-to books from scripting and writing to directing to costuming to film technique. If you're *in the biz* and need to promote a play, advertise an acting class, or announce an audition, your fliers and cards are welcome.

Most importantly, this bookstore has been a vital hub for the performing arts community since 1917, attracting everyone from students to stars. Bulletin boards post events and casting calls. A performance space in the basement hosts rehearsals (*In the Heights* started here!), lectures by luminaries, and workshops. DBS is a haven for the steady stream of actors flowing through, perusing their floor-to-ceiling shelves in search of a theatrical epiphany. The shop is inviting and nurturing. There are seating areas for comfy reading, and strains of show-tunes play on weekends. A truly dedicated Help Desk to assist in finding just the right audition monologue or where to repair tap shoes. For its supreme value to the performing arts community it was awarded an honorary Tony in 2011 for "excellence in theater." It's *that* good.

For stage, film, or television, the Drama Book Shop is the holy grail of learning for the theatrical artist. Once inside, you will know instantly whether you wish *to be or not to be* part of this singular experience.

Address 250 West 40th Street (near Eighth Avenue), New York 10018, Phone
+1 212.944.0595, www.dramabookshop.com, info@dramabookshop.com | Transit
Subway: 42 St-Times Sq (1, 2, 3, 7, A, C, E, N, Q, R); 42 St-Bryant Park (B, D, F, M),
Bus: M 7, M 11, M 20, M 34, M 42, M 104 | Hours Mon–Wed, Fri, Sat 11am–7pm,
Thurs 11am–8pm, Sun 12–6pm

28__East Village Cheese
A surprising transcendence

The first thing you notice about this storefront just down the street from Cooper Union is that it looks more like a bulletin board than a window display, with dozens of handwritten signs highlighting specials of the week. Once inside the bustling cash-only shop, you're flanked by open refrigerated cases stocked with delectable sale items – brie, feta, parmesan, domestic and foreign cheeses, sausages, and yogurts – all at unexpectedly low prices. Further along is a select choice of fresh breads, baguettes, bagels, quiches, and coffee beans.

Opposite is the soul of the shop: an open counter with an impressive assortment of cheeses from around the world. Brie and gouda are the most popular, but you'll also find buttery Danish Blue Castello, aromatic Morbier, and Finnish Lappi. They carry an array of other foods to complement cheese, such as olives, cold cuts, crackers, dried fruits, and condiments.

The original owner, Al Kaufman, was a convert from Judaism to Buddhism. During the nineties he employed several Tibetan exiles, former Buddhist monks, who had fled their country to escape the Chinese occupation and oppression. One had been jailed for displaying a picture of the Tibetan flag. The immigrants first worked in the back of the store cutting cheese. As they became more proficient in English, they also learned the trade.

The Tibetans' gentle and humble manner – tracing back to their training as monks – inspired Kaufman. When he decided to retire in 2005, he offered the business to two of them, Thupten Tenphel and Lobsang Tsultrim. In order to accept the offer, they had to relinquish their vows in the process. "It's hard to be a monk in America," said Tenphel. They haven't changed a thing about either the cheese selection, the caring customer service, or the nondescript interior. The space is the same, but there is a new awareness informed by a higher, and ancient, spiritual tradition.

Address 40 Third Avenue (near 9th Street), New York 10003, **Phone** +1 212.477.2601 |
Transit Subway: Astor Pl (6); 8 St-NYU (N, R); Union Sq-14 St (4, 5, 6, 6X); 3rd Ave (L),
Bus: M 1, M 2, M 3, M 8, M 101, M 102, M 103 | **Hours** Daily 8:30am – 6:30pm

29___Eataly NYC

A nonstop feast, Italian style

In the shadow of the Flatiron Building is New York's trendiest Italian food emporium. Inside this cavernous, labyrinthine hall, the air buzzes with energy and excitement. Meandering strollers ooh and aah, pausing at every turn to inhale a tantalizing aroma or admire one of the tempting food displays. They explore the endless nooks that punctuate the aisles with different specialties. It's organized chaos – and great fun the whole way.

Eataly – a modern-day food bazaar – invites curious tasters to sample a multitude of Italian delights for an exciting eating adventure. Shop, taste, and savor top-quality traditional dishes, locally grown produce, and artisanal treats. The multifunctional marketplace has retail shops for prime meats, fish, cold cuts, cheeses, vegetables, Italian delicacies, and fine wines; a diverse slate of cafes and boutique eateries; and a learning center with cooking classes and demonstrations. The enthusiastic staff aims to please, whether you're shopping for dinner, stopping by for a snack, or enjoying a full-course, sit-down meal.

Lunch or dinner at one of the nine restaurants features authentic dishes, each with a different culinary emphasis, and situated near the retail areas providing their fresh ingredients: Le Verdure is next to the produce section; La Piazza by the cheese and cold cuts counter; Il Pesce by the fishmonger; La Pizza & La Pasta at the bakery; Manzo's menu of meats near the butcher. Pranzo's light lunch is served in La Scuola, the cooking classroom. I Panini has a selection of freshly made sandwiches. Rosticceria serves eat-in or take-out roasted meats, rotisserie chicken, and assorted antipasti. And the rooftop restaurant and brewery, Birreria, features its own cask ales, hardy pub food, and knockout skyline vistas.

Eataly is a state-of-the-art, not-to-be missed food experience, Italian style. Let your senses lead the way – and *mangia, mangia!*

Address 200 Fifth Avenue (near 23rd Street), New York 10010, Phone +1 212.229.2560, www.eataly.com, customerservice@eataly.com | Transit Subway: 23 St (N, R, F, M, 6), Bus: M 1, M 2, M 3, M 5, M 7, M 23 | Hours Daily 10am–11pm

ITALY
IS
EATALY

YOU ARE
WHAT YOU
EATALY

30 Economy Candy
Sweet memories

Gourmet magazine described this real-world Candyland as "the penny-candy store elevated to an art form." A Lower East Side treasure since 1937, Economy Candy was originally a shoe store that sold candy over the counter. When candy began outselling shoes, a transition was made.

Prepare to be overwhelmed. It's a wellspring of variety and abundance. Bulk bins teem with familiar, and sometimes exotic, tastes and textures: sour, sweet, tart, sticky, soft, hard, fruity, nutty. Let your eye wander and you'll spot museum-worthy antique toys, games, signs, candy wrappers, boxes, and tins. It's a time-machine trip to early twentieth-century pop culture.

The store is packed floor to ceiling, and stepping through the doors is like a blast from the past with the sweet smell of over 2,000 varieties of candies, chocolates, dried fruits, and nuts. If Economy doesn't have what you're looking for, they probably don't make it anymore. From Abba Zabas to Zero Bars, you'll find every candy from your childhood – and your parents' too – Mary Janes, Tootsie Rolls, Skybars, Pixy Stix, Big Hunks, Atomic Fireballs, Ring Pops, Pop Rocks, Bonomos Turkish Taffy, Astro Pops, and Pez. There are also gummy bears (plus fish, worms, and other chewable critters), whistle pops, jelly beans, all-day suckers bigger than your head, candy berries, buttons, jawbreakers, sourballs, chocolate-covered apricots, chocolate eggs, Tabasco-flavored candy, wine gums, candy cigarettes, and bacon mints. Sugar-free and low-cal candies, gift baskets, and hand-dipped chocolates were added to the selection to reflect the changing urban landscape.

'Youngsters' of 1937 are not too old to stop by for a scoopful of goodies or hard-to-find imported brands. The owners Jerry and Mitch Cohen say some regulars even bring in empty suitcases to stuff with sugary delights. On Halloween, the store gives away a truckload of candy. One catch – you gotta be a kid!

Address 108 Rivington Street (near Essex Street), New York 10002, Phone +1 212.254.1531, www.economycandy.com | Transit Subway: Delancey St (F); Essex St (J, M), Bus: M 9, M 14A, M 15, M 21 | Hours Mon 10am–6pm, Tue–Fri 9am–6pm, Sat 10am–5pm, Sun 9am–6pm

31 Eight of Swords Tattoo
Get inked, and then some

Williamsburg has the kind of rebellious creative energy the East Village was famous for in its early days. The neighborhood nurtures an artist population and provides a sense of close community. These elements all come together at Eight of Swords, which is not just a tattoo parlor, or an art gallery, or a crafts boutique. It's all of the above, located in the charming storefront of an 1840s house. The owner is veteran tattoo artist David Wallin, who inks in a wide range of styles. Along with other skilled tattooists, both local and international, Wallin brings his clients' visions and stories to life through beautifully detailed work. In the ambience of a Victorian parlour, Eight of Swords' spacious, clean, relaxing environment creates a comfortable atmosphere to discuss and visualize ideas, then transform them into customized body art.

At the front of the shop is a choice boutique featuring apothecary and grooming items, and handcrafted jewelry and adornments made by talented local designers. These unusual works in silver, gold, leather, and bronze make exceptional and affordable gifts.

The studio's art gallery showcases emerging and established artists from around the world. The work is variously evocative, outsider, lowbrow, controversial, beautiful, ugly, and cutting edge. With its high-energy parties, gallery openings draw neighbors and visitors alike – a great opportunity to meet fascinating people and buy original artworks.

You can turn your trip from Manhattan to Eight of Swords into an adventure. Apart from subway or bus, there's also the nearby East River Ferry landing at N 6th Street (accessed from midtown at E 34th Street or downtown at Wall Street). Or enjoy panoramic city views by taking the Williamsburg Bridge walkway, accessible from Delancey Street. However you go, Eight of Swords is a triple treat. Take a boat ride or bridge-walk across the river and see for yourself.

Address 115 Grand Street (near Bedford Avenue), Brooklyn 11249, Phone +1 718.387.9673, www.8ofswords.com, info@8ofswords.com | Transit Subway: Bedford Ave (L), Bus: B 32, B 62 | Hours Wed–Mon 12–8pm

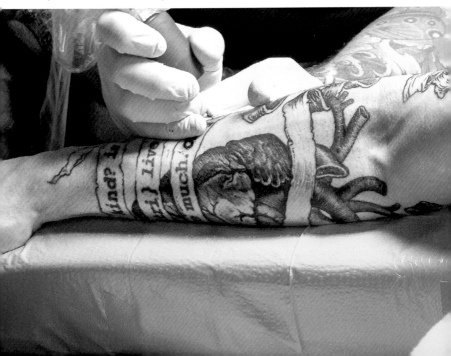

32 The Eloise Shop
A sweet at The Plaza

Eloise, the beloved fictional nuisance of The Plaza who terrorized hotel staff and guests alike with her mischievous antics, now has a retail shop in the very place she calls home. She is rich, spoiled, parent-free (with a "rawther" British nanny, her "mostly companion"), and runs wild in the poshest hotel in New York.

This capricious 6-year-old came to life in 1955 on the pages of the first of four books written by Kay Thompson, a flamboyant musical performer who was a resident of the hotel. Eloise has since lodged herself in the hearts of generations of little girls who would love nothing more than to be her. Illustrator Hilary Knight gave her a pot belly, patent leather Mary-Janes, and a big pink bow in her hair. She does as she pleases and lives by the motto "being bored is not allowed." Who wouldn't want to be her? Adults included.

It's not certain if Eloise was the alter-ego of the author, or if the precocious city kid was modeled after goddaughter Liza Minelli (Thompson was close friends with Judy Garland). But the mystique has lasted for over half a century. Breathing life into fiction, the staff at The Plaza are in on the ruse and will courteously pander to little girls visiting to experience it firsthand. The doorman may tip his hat to your princess as you enter the crystal-chandeliered lobby with the famous Palm Court (where Eloise "loves, loves, loves" to dine).

On the lower level, The Shop carries all things Eloise, mostly drenched in her favorite color, pink. The branded merchandise is set in a splendid fantasy world infused with details from the book. Your angel can sit at Eloise's vanity table, tickle the keys of her pink mini-piano, prance about her dressing room, throw a pretend tea party, or perform on stage. And yes, they do birthday parties.

Indulge the spoiled brat in your little darling (and your own inner child). It will be a treat for both of you.

Address The Plaza Hotel, Lower Level, Fifth Avenue at Central Park South (59th Street), New York 10019, Phone +1 212.546.5460, www.theplazany.com/shops/eloise-at-the-plaza, eloise@theplaza.com | Transit Subway: 5th Ave-59 St (N, Q, R); 59 St-Lexington Ave (4, 5, 6); 57 St (F); 5th Ave-53 St (E, M), Bus: M1, M2, M3, M4, M5, M7, M20, M31, M57, M66, M72, M101, M102, M103 | Hours Mon−Sat 11am−8pm, Sun 11am−6pm

33 — Enchantments

Knowing which is witch

Enchantments is one of the most *magical* shops in the city. Billed as "New York's oldest occult store," they've been creating potions and lotions to ward off evil spirits and conjure good luck since 1982. Weave among the altars brimming with items to help fulfill your desires – oils, herbals and botanicals, incense, charms and talismans, candles, and jewelry. Enchantments can provide astrology, tarot, and psychic readings; instruction in creating and casting candle-spells; and supplies to practitioners of witchcraft and other sacred rituals, including wiccan.

There are candles galore, from the 7-day pillar – carved with magical symbols, your name, and zodiac sign – to figurines of man, woman, or animal, to simple votive, coach, and taper styles. Find candles intended for healing, blessing, love, luck, or success. Explore your own witchy fantasies – take a class and create your own herb- and glitter-infused spell-casting wax beauties. Their resident Wizard, working stealthily behind a counter at the back, whips up magic from a stock formulary with hundreds of recipes for custom-blended fragrant and essential oils, herbs and resins, powder incense, and bath oils. Personal readings address spiritual evolution with tarot, chakra work, yoga, reiki, fitness, nutrition, and magic to achieve a balance of mind, body, and spirit.

The staff, well-versed in the ways of the occult, provides careful guidance in the mystical arts, offering a selection of books to assist both the novice and the more experienced practitioner. The latter will also find tools of the trade – cauldrons, chalices, and pentacles. Don't be surprised to see cats prowling about, bewitching the browsers – one just might curl purringly around your ankles.

You'll be enchanted by items crafted by local artists: one-of-a-kind jewelry, handpainted note cards; hand-carved rune sets of stone or naturally shed deer antler; wands made of ethically harvested wood. This is one-stop shopping for pagans of all kinds.

Address 424 East 9th Street (near First Avenue), New York 10009, Phone +1 212.228.4394, www.enchantmentsincnyc.com, enchantmentsny@gmail.com | Transit Subway: 1st Ave (L); Astor Pl (6); 8 St (N, R); 2nd Ave (F), Bus: M1, M3, M9, M14, M15, M21, M102, M103 | Hours Wed–Mon 1–9pm

34__The Evolution Store

Scorpion lollipop, anyone?

Ever wish you could reach into one of the displays at the Museum of Natural History and take home a really amazing souvenir? A 10,000-year-old bear skull? A stuffed armadillo? A raccoon-penis bone? You can do just that at a fantastic museum-like shop on a bustling street in Soho called The Evolution Store.

Since 1993 this two-story oddities emporium, jam-packed with nature's marvels and curios, has been selling an eye-popping assortment of taxidermy, insects, skulls, skeletons, fossils, seashells, stones, and minerals. Some are artifacts, others replicas. Gift choices range from the expected to the outrageous – beautiful and quirky jewelry, chic home accessories, animal-skin rugs, anatomical models, puzzles and games, candied bugs, poison-frog purses, and copulating skeletons.

Owner and curator William Stevens' passion for entomology, paleontology, and anthropology is what drives The Evolution Store. When he and a team of experts and professionals are not scouring the globe for exotic rarities, Stevens is in the shop chatting with customers about his incredible finds. All items are legally obtained from scientists and private collectors.

Some things on display are heart-stoppers: the cobra coiled to strike; a menacing giant bear skeleton; the ferocious lion set to pounce. Keep looking and you'll see collections of shrunken heads, intricately carved skulls, and terrifying tribal masks. Mesmerized kids roam the store in wide-eyed wonder. Bug enthusiasts can spend hours ogling thousands of exquisite entomology specimens from beetles to butterflies, and even join up for an entomology workshop. Evolution's artisans can custom-design framed or glass-domed insects to your specifications.

The gregarious, well-informed staff encourages browsing and assists customers with every inquiry, no matter how off-the-wall. Treat yourself to an exciting trip into the twilight zone of scientific history.

Address 120 Spring Street (near Mercer Street), New York 10012, Phone +1 212.343.1114, www.theevolutionstore.com, info@theevolutionstore.com | Transit Subway: Prince St (N, R); Spring St (6, C, E); Broadway-Lafayette (B, D, F, M), Bus: M5, M21 | Hours Daily 11am–7pm

35 Fabulous Fanny's Eyewear

Here's looking at you, kid

If you don't have 20/20 vision – rejoice! Now you have a perfect excuse to run amok at Fabulous Fanny's, whose motto is: *If you have to wear them, make it fun.* And what fun it is!

This East Village emporium, with over 30,000 frames in their inventory, offers a cornucopian collection of eyewear from as far back as the 1700s, covering centuries of beautiful, playful, odd, and flamboyant vintage eye frames – right up to today's hippest styles (represented by their own brand, aptly named Spectaculars). You'll find all shapes and all materials – cat's eye, wraparound, oval, square, granny, aviator, rhinestone, horn-rimmed, and gold-wire. Using an unusual sales approach, most of the merchandise is held in accessible, antique wooden drawers labeled for easy reference. You are encouraged to rummage through them and try on as many frames as you'd like in order to find that unique connection to your own iconic image.

Opened in 2001, Fabulous Fanny's quickly became a destination boutique – a mecca for any who appreciate the history, design, and esthetics of eyewear. You'll be gaga over the one-of-a-kind spectacles on exhibit in their mini-museum — among them, bicycle-shaped frames and Harry Potter's eyeglass case.

Besides eyewear, curated vintage clothing and accessories are artfully displayed in themed vignettes throughout the store. It's a pleasure just to wander about. A whimsical selection of women's hats dating back to the 1930s will make you smile, along with old-style clothing and costume jewelry. And you'll also find one of the best assortments of vintage men's accessories, featuring bow ties, pocket squares, suspenders, hats, and cufflinks.

This lighthearted shop makes it a point to have something affordable for everybody. So try on as many as you like – you're bound to find The Look you've always longed for.

Address 335 East 9th Street (near First Avenue), New York 10003, Phone +1 212.533.0637, www.fabulousfannys.com, fanny@fabulousfannys.com | Transit Subway: 1st Ave (L); Astor Pl (6); 8 St-NYU (N, R); 2nd Ave (F), Bus: M1, M2, M3, M5, M8, M14, M15, M101, M102, M103 | Hours Daily 12–8pm

36 Faerman Cash Registers
Ker-ching, ker-ching – music to the ear

What goes around, comes around. There was a time when the Bowery was shrouded by an elevated subway, and a section of what was then 'skid row' was known as the cash register district – home to a dozen-odd stores selling and repairing big-bellied instruments of money collection. Originally invented to prevent employees from pilfering the profits (that's why they had bells), cash registers are back in vogue as ornate artifacts of a bygone era. With only one cash register store left in Manhattan, it appears that holding on to something that you've grown to love pays off in the long run; sales of these reconditioned machines – working antiques – are on the rise.

Brian Faerman, son of nonagenarian Bernard (and grandson of the original 1910 owner), runs this shop not only *with* his dad, but *for* his dad. "It's all about him," says Brian, glancing over at his gray-haired, beaming father, who reminisces with customers about the old days, how machines today are not what they used to be – well-crafted, built to last. "Things are made cheap now," laments papa Bernard, who has spent much of his life tinkering inside the metallic guts of cash registers, adjusting the gears and repairing the bells that he says have become "music to my ears." (Can't you hear Pink Floyd's *Money* playing in the background?)

The store is lined with row upon row of expertly restored, shiny vintage models, still capable of delivering a wicked stomach punch when the till flies open! Selling for thousands of dollars each, they're sought after by a new breed of clientele for chic restaurants, bars, and trendy shops.

In an age of sophisticated *devices* and endless innovations, it's refreshing when something old has more appeal than something new. The intricate design, majestic presence, and untold stories hidden inside their cash drawers are truly a trip to the past. Or is it a nostalgic trip to the future?

Address 159 Bowery (near Broome Street), New York 10002, Phone +1 212.226.2935, faermancashregister@gmail.com | Transit Subway: Bowery (J); Grand St (B, D); Spring St (6), Bus: M 15, M 21, M 103 | Hours Mon – Fri 9am – 5pm, Sat 9am – 2pm

37 Fishs Eddy

A dishy shop for tasteful servers

A one-of-a-kind store in New York, Fishs Eddy serves up the wares for carrying, containing, and presenting food: dinnerware, flatware, glassware, kitchenware, and of course serveware. What makes the shop so unique is its excellently priced vintage dishes – relics of bygone ocean liners, defunct restaurants and clubs, manufacturers' closeouts, and odd lots. The decidedly un-urban, rustic, ramshackle atmosphere feels like a country tag sale. Everywhere you look are old barrels, cabinets, and baskets brimming over with goodies – a banquet of choices, even before the food hits the table!

It all started in 1986 when the owners were driving around the back roads of upstate New York and came upon a charming hamlet with the odd name of Fishs Eddy – an irresistible appellation for their newly opened shop in Manhattan. As they bounced through the countryside in their dented old blue pick-up truck, they began scouring for interesting finds.

One of the earliest was in an old barn being used to store dishware from a nearby manufacturer. Filled with plates, bowls, cups, and saucers, the barn had been in a serious fire. But, remarkably, every single soot-covered dish was still intact – although solid black, with no discernable pattern. The adventuring owners purchased the whole lot and hauled it back to the city where they meticulously scrubbed each piece. They soon realized they had discovered dishware with patterns and shapes that were beautiful and truly classic – a real slice of American history. They knew they were on to something special. They brought their treasure to the store – and customers agreed! This was their future.

Fishs Eddy carries gazillions of edgy and fun dishes, glasses, tableware, many displayed by theme (like New York Skyline). The owners still comb unexplored places for unexpected finds. And after all these years, they still love 'doing dishes'!

Address 889 Broadway (at 19th Street), New York 10003, Phone +1 212.420.9020, www.fishseddy.com, info@fishseddy.com | **Transit** Subway: 14 St-Union Sq (L, N, Q, R); 23 St (N, R), Bus: M 1, M 3, M 23 | **Hours** Mon 10am–9pm, Tue–Sat 9am–9pm, Sun 10am–8pm

38 Forbidden Planet

Pure NYC nerd-vana

It's no accident that from out on the street at lower Broadway you can see the glittering cavernous interior of this pop-culture emporium. It was designed to lure you into the fantasy world of superhero merchandise from pre-Superman to anime to Battlestar Galactica and beyond. Lining the walls end-to-end are comics both current and vintage, compilations of old and soon-to-be classics, reprints, zines, dvd's, board and video games, logo t-shirts, gadgets, and all manner of geek paraphernalia. There are aisles of graphic novels, reference books, and collections in every category of comics and science fiction, rare and limited editions of books, posters, art, and other collectibles.

Themed display cases are filled with brilliantly-colored action figures, superhero memorabilia with a wide assortment of American classics like Wonder Woman, Spiderman, Batman, X-Men, plus Japanese anime figures, manga, Hot Toys, bobbleheads, Funko heroes, Star Wars characters, and the list goes on. It's a transportive experience to get lost amidst the bizarre fictional worlds these characters inhabit.

The original Forbidden Planet started out as a small comics shop in London in 1978. Its founders joined forces with owners of a similar enterprise in Edinburgh and eventually Forbidden Planet International emerged, creating the iconic New York store and others. Fans and passersby drop in and spend hours leisurely browsing the shelves, sharing anecdotes and insider gossip, and asking questions of the admittedly geeky staff, all of whom are, by definition, totally tuned-in devotees of the genre. A rush of regular customers appears every Wednesday when the new releases of comics arrive.

The staff is, as one enthusiast remarked, "insanely helpful and knowledgeable." One clerk said he'd been asking the owner for a job there ever since he was eight years old "because I just always wanted to be there."

Address 832 Broadway (near 13th Street), New York 10003, Phone +1 212.473.1576,
www.fpnyc.com | Transit Subway: Union Sq-14 St (4, 5, 6, 6X, L, N, Q, R), Bus: M1,
M2, M3, M5, M8, M14, M101, M102, M103 | Hours Sun–Tue 9am–10pm, Wed–Sat
9am–midnight

39 Fountain Pen Hospital

The pen is mightier than the keyboard

If you think fountain pens have gone the way of typewriters and vinyl records, think again. They're back. Fountain Pen Hospital is a thriving business today thanks to a global marketplace. In this internet age where we 'write' on touchpads, there's still a demand. Politicians, professionals, executives, students, and tourists alike are drawn to this Wall Street area shop to resurrect the nostalgic practice of personal, expressive writing – a forgotten art once known as penmanship. And a finely made pen, responsive and sensitive to the touch, says what no keyboard can.

Fountain Pen Hospital has one of the largest collections of classic, vintage, and new pens anywhere, and is the only shop of its kind in America. Prices go from $20 to $12,000, depending on its material – copper, steel, leather, gold, precious gems, even lava stone. The oldest pen in the store dates to 1910 and is made of 18-karat gold. Some commemorative limited editions even contain actual bits of history, like a piece of the first manned spaceship to the moon in 1969, embedded in the pen itself.

In 1946 the Wiederlight family opened a repair shop, a hospital for writing instruments. With the advent of cheap ballpoints in the seventies, fountain pens began fading into obscurity. The business expanded to general office supplies until the big chains swallowed up that market.

In a bold move, they returned to their roots, sensing an appetite for retro pen-and-ink. The founder's grandsons still retain the word Hospital as an homage to the past, although most of their business is now in retail sales. The brothers are proud of the store's many celebrity patrons over the years – Ernest Hemingway, Betty Grable, Count Basie, and many others.

Today we can text, tweet, and email to get our message across, but there's no doubt that a personal handwritten note – a rarity today – says more than just the words on the page.

Address 10 Warren Street (near Broadway), New York 10007, Phone +1 212.964.0580, www.fountainpenhospital.com, info@fountainpenhospital.com | Transit Subway: City Hall (R); Chambers St (A, C, J, 1); Park Place (2, 3); Brooklyn Bridge (4, 5, 6); World Trade Center (E), Bus: M 9, M 20, M 22, M 103 | Hours Mon–Fri 7:45am–5:30pm

On July 20, 1969, "...one small step for man, one giant leap for mankind..." Humans achieved a dream of standing on ... history to walk on th... The spacecraft which carried Neil and me to the Moon was ... symbolic name *Columbia*. To protect our fragile craft from t... of material known as **KAPTON FOIL**, gold-colored on the f... outside skin of the *Columbia*. This delicate foil played a critica... ship, helping us to maintain comfortable temperatures within. B... the *Columbia*, its gold-colored side was directly exposed to dee...

...the extremely fragile nature of the foil, most of it burned ... into ...th's atmosphere on July 24, 1969. However, a small p... Ame... ...kwell Recovery Team on board the aircraft carrier H... Rockw... prime manufacturer of the *Columbia*. Krone Pen... eternity ...ting it in their special edition pen.

When re... ...chal voyage of Apollo 11, I often think of ... ...nquillity ...Ba... inscription HERE MEN FROM THE P... ...ON THE ...E IN PEACE FOR ALL MANKIND. ...a defining m... ...olution, when mankind lifted itself f... ...ry into the un...

40__ Garber Hardware

If I had a hammer ...

This place is a modern-day throwback to the good old days. When you first step into the deceptively large space, you're struck by the familiar sights and smells of the old-style local hardware store – with its maze-like aisles and cul-de-sacs lined with bins of screws, nuts, bolts, and nails; shelves loaded with tools, household lumber, paints, plastics, and lubricants; spools of wire, rope, and chain; electrical supplies, plumbing parts, gardening tools, and kitchen gadgets.

Displaced in the last few decades by mega-stores like Home Depot, these family-owned shops are a dying breed. But here, almost camouflaged on a scenic street in the West Village, you can take a step back in time. Interestingly, the traditional neighborhood hardware store has survived best in big cities, where residents prefer to step outside their apartments and conveniently walk a few blocks to their local shop.

One of the most outstanding of the neighborhood hardware stores is surely Garber's, many times voted 'Best Hardware Store' in the city – not only for its enormous selection of inventory, but also its longstanding reputation for dispensing friendly, expert advice. A rare service these days.

Founded in 1884 by Joseph Garber, a Russian immigrant, the store stands now as one of the oldest family-owned and operated businesses *of any kind* in New York City. Originally selling only paint and paint products, it expanded over the decades into its current array of hardware and housewares – items as varied as massive metal hooks, roller blinds, real straw brooms, reusable ice-pop molds, and multi-pocketed canvas tool bags – an efficient, even stylish, alternative to bulky plastic or metal toolboxes. All of these special items are supplemented by their endless list of standard hardware items. Indeed, this unique store has no problem living up to its motto: *Garber's has everything!*

Address 710 Greenwich Street (near 10th Street), New York 10014, Phone
+1 212.929.3030, www.garberhardware.com, sales@garberhardware.com | Transit Subway:
Christopher St-Sheridan Sq (1); West 4 St (A, B, C, D, E, F, M), Bus: M2, M8, M11,
M14A | Hours Mon–Thurs 8am–8pm, Fri–Sat 8am–5pm, Sun 10am–4pm

41 Gem Spa

Home of New York's best egg cream

Beat poet Allen Ginsberg dubbed it the 'nerve center' of the city. At the peak of its notoriety in the 1960s, the weekly *Village Voice* called it "the official oasis of the East Village" – a hippie hangout where protests were organized amidst the mingled aroma of marijuana and incense. Later, Gem Spa became a punk-scene mecca for the most strident display of exhibitionism: day-glo mohawks, wildly colorful tattoos, body-piercing, studded leather, shredded and safety-pinned clothes, and goth makeup. Today Gem Spa continues to lure curious young people from all over – those who are still seeking self-expression and espousing anti-establishment values. Tourists pass by, many of them to stop and stare.

Sitting on the bustling corner of St. Marks Place and Second Avenue, this 24/7 newsstand and magazine shop still sells underground papers, hundreds of different periodicals, cigarettes, and drug-culture paraphernalia. But times have changed and the busy corner has become much more commercial, with stalls of NYC souvenirs, logo hats, sunglasses, and cheap trendy accessories crowding the once-iconic corner.

The classic egg cream was once a delicate mainstay of soda fountains throughout New York, but is now mostly history. Except at Gem Spa, where its famous trademark remains alive and bubbly – a soda fountain drink comprising milk, seltzer, and either chocolate or vanilla syrup. (There is no cream and no egg in an egg cream!) The magical blend of these ingredients – along with the technique for combining them in a tall glass – is still a well-guarded secret. But simple observation reveals several squirts of syrup into the bottom of the glass, the addition of a small amount of milk, followed by a highly pressurized jet of seltzer. The mixture is carefully blended with a long spoon, creating an overflowing head of foam. Years of practice tell the man behind the counter exactly when to stop, handing the concoction over to the customer. Get ready for a unique taste treat that is traditional New York, and "the very best"!

Address 131 Second Avenue (at St Marks Place), New York 10003, Phone +1 212.529.1146 | Transit Subway: Astor Pl (6); 8 St-NYU (N, R); Union Sq (4, 6, 6X); 3rd Ave (L), Bus: M 8, M 15, M 101, M 102, M 103 | Hours Daily 24 hours

42 Gotham Model Trains

Where the old are on track with the young

Tucked away on the 13th floor of an unassuming building in the garment district, Gotham is one of a few remaining shops in the city devoted specifically to railroad hobbyists. Other places diversify into other modeling realms, but for dedicated railroad buffs this is mecca. Their broad selection of model trains and accessories – in track gauges from O to Z – appeals to everyone's ageless imagination, from wide-eyed beginner to veteran modeler. Here it's not uncommon to see an 80-year-old grandpa and an 8-year-old kid sharing the finer points of a caboose's detailing or their favorite miniature scenery pieces. From a basic starter train set to vintage custom-made brass locomotives, there's something enticing for all generations.

Gotham's stock of diminutive buildings, figures, vehicles, and scenery attracts model-makers and craftspeople from a wide range of backgrounds and lifestyles, and they 'talk shop' with each other as they browse. An architect crafting a scale model of future Manhattan skyscrapers chats with a hip Brooklynite building a terrarium; a mom and daughter working on a school project get ideas from a videographer doing an animation sequence or a visual artist constructing a piece for a gallery installation.

Whether you're building your own railroad empire at home or looking for inspiration from the countless miniature objects to apply to another type of project, Gotham specializes in bringing dreams to reality through the lilliputian world of scale modeling.

Browsing their selection of shiny new and collectible vintage items, it's easy to feel the lure of this hobby. In today's world of addictive video games and irresistible apps, model railroading has a special appeal for many enthusiasts – it's a relaxing escape from our internet-obsessed culture, a reminder of days gone by and simpler times, when ages eight and eighty had more in common.

All aboard!

Address 224 West 35th Street, 13th floor (near Seventh Avenue), New York 10001, Phone +1 212.643.4400, www.gothammodeltrains.com, mail@gothammodeltrains.com | **Transit** Subway: 34 St-Penn Sta (A, C, E, 1, 2, 3); 34 St-Herald Sq (B, D, F, M, N, Q, R), Bus: M 1, M 3, M 4, M 5, M 7, M 11, M 20, M 34, M 104 | **Hours** Mon–Fri 11am–6pm, Sat 11am–5pm

43 Gothic Renaissance

Deliciously ghoulish fashion-goulash

Need just the right lacy knuckle-gloves to wear with your studded stiletto boots? Or maybe a titillating Victorian choker to complement your silky steampunk bustier? You're an avid GothLolita or a Twilight-inspired vampire? Look no further and head downtown to Gothic Renaissance. They can outfit you from head to toe, from hats to hosiery. No shop in the city offers more of a selection or variety of these elaborately tailored clothes and accessories.

Goth culture stems from the late-seventies rock scene, encompassing postpunk, new wave, cyberpunk, glamrock, deathrock, darkwave, industrial music, and more. World-famous designers like Alexander McQueen, Jean-Paul Gaultier, and John Galliano have catapulted Goth into mainstream fashion over the past few decades.

Even if you don't know the origins of the movement or the names of the trending designers, you'll find a visit to this cave-like emporium a fascinating downtown stop. Clientele range from young people looking for affordable, alternative styles to collectors willing to shell out for one-of-a-kind pieces, with prices from $20 to $2,500. Floor-to-ceiling racks and shelves are crammed with apparel of all sorts for men and women – corsets, coats, capes, lace, leather, velvet dresses, boots, shoes, masks, studded and feathered accessories. Plus zipper-lined pants, vinyl skirts, lingerie, fetish underwear, handmade jewelry, hair accessories, and make-up. The mask collection is dazzling – from exquisite Venetian creations to inexpensive imitations. There's even a book section devoted to Goth culture.

Before you leave, go next door to New York Costumes, where you can indulge every other imaginable dress-up fantasy. Browsing there is like walking through an amusement park funhouse. The same owners have two full floors with thousands of costumes, masks, accessories, and make-up.

Between the two stores, you can spend a whole day in fantasyland!

Address 110 Fourth Avenue (near Union Square), New York 10003, Phone +1 212.780.9558, www.gothren.com, gothicrenaissancenyc@gmail.com | Transit Subway: Union Sq-14 St (4, 5, 6, 6X, L, N, Q, R); Bus: M 1, M 2, M 3, M 5, M 8, M 14A, M 14D, M 101, M 102, M 103n | Hours Mon–Sat 11am–8pm, Sun 12–7pm

44 Greenwich Street Cookbooks

For the tasteful bibliophile

This quaint shop (aka Joanne Hendricks, Cookbooks) tucked away in a quiet corner west of Soho, carries a broad spectrum of out-of-print, vintage, and unusual culinary books. Look for the old sandwich board sign outside a weathered wooden door, its brass plaque bearing the single word Cookbooks. The cozy shop occupies the ground-floor front of a landmark 1823 Federal-style brick building. Hendricks and her family have lived there since they purchased it in 1975, opening the shop in 1995.

Inside is everything from recipe collections by various authors of different eras, to volumes on all things food-related – entertaining, etiquette, holiday cuisine, famous chefs, notorious restaurants, memoirs, biographies, even works of fiction where food plays a major role in the plot. No fad-diet menu or trendy compendia here – just a mouth-watering stew of old classics, rare titles, and hard-to-find first editions by authors like Alice B. Toklas, MFK Fisher, Julia Child, Alice Waters, Ruth Reichl, Paul Prudhomme, James Beard, to mention a noteworthy few. The treasured, most-fragile books – many with beautiful cover art and illustrations – are in good condition, protected in plastic sleeves. Not limited to English-language, Greenwich Street Cookbooks dishes up lovingly curated books from around the world. An estimated 900 titles crowd the antique cabinets and floor-to-ceiling shelves.

Perched here and there around the shop's timeworn library is an eclectic array of kitchen and table curios. A children's tea set, a cast iron pot, dainty demitasse cups, bone china saucers, and yellowing posters, prints, photographs, and menus. Prices are fair, depending on an item's rarity. It's a wonderful shop for leisurely browsing – or to pick up a unique, affordable gift for that special gourmet in your life without going hungry yourself. It's deliciously gastronomical, and not necessarily astronomical.

Address 488 Greenwich Street (near Canal Street), New York 10013, Phone +1 212.226.5731, www.greenwichstreetcookbooks.com, joannehendricks@gmail.com | Transit Subway: Canal St (A, 1); Spring St (C, E), Bus: M5, M20, M21 | Hours Daily 11:30am–7pm

45 Happy Chopsticks

Not just tools, but folklore

Happy Chopsticks, a serene oasis in the midst of cacophonous Chinatown, at first glance looks like a jewelry store. Look again and you realize you're seeing elegant, slender sticks, like graceful fingers, gently propped against the satin backing of brocade gift boxes all along the walls and antique tables. Chopsticks are the traditional eating utensils of China, Japan, Korea, Indonesia, and Vietnam. Originating in ancient China and used first as cooking tools, they were commonly made of bamboo, bone, or metal. Over the centuries, as food was later prepared in smaller, bite-sized pieces, chopsticks were adapted for dining as well, and were crafted of jade, porcelain, and luxury materials like ivory (now banned), sterling silver, and gold.

Yunhong Chopsticks, a well-established chain with over fifty outlets in China, opened its first US franchise in 2008. This tiny boutique displays hundreds of choices, from traditional to modern, with good luck symbols or historical themes like Mao's sayings. Priced for anyone's budget – from $1.99 for plain plastic to $600 for gold leaf or lacquered black ebony that are destined to become family heirlooms – you'll find novel gifts like *I ♥ New York* or Chinese zodiac sets, or starter chopsticks for children. Others are carved or elaborately engraved, some inlaid with seashells. Many come with 'stands' for laying down chopsticks between bites. Each set has its own story and decorative gift-box.

Get expert advice on technique, etiquette, and care – and learn fascinating facts and lore. Did you know that the shape and length of chopsticks differ from one culture to another? That the Chinese word for chopsticks sounds like "happiness" – so giving them as a gift is like bestowing a blessing. And, more dramatically, that silver-tipped chopsticks were once used to test food because it was believed that the silver would turn black on contact with poison!

Address 50 Mott Street (near Bayard Street), New York 10013, Phone +1 212.566.8828, www.happychopsticks.com, email@happychopsticks.com | Transit Subway: Canal St (J, N, Q, R, 6), Bus: M 9, M 22, M 103 | Hours Daily 10:30am – 8:30pm

46 Housing Works Bookstore Cafe

A store where you feel at home

Take pleasure in just being here. Something in the air warms the soul and somehow relieves stress when you enter the vast, balconied space. This richly wood-lined, high-ceilinged, library-style bookstore cafe has established itself as a relevant downtown institution, staffed almost entirely by volunteers. The walls are stacked with used books gifted by caring donors. It's a great spot to meet friends, relax, and take advantage of the irresistible bargains in one of the best book, movie, and music selections in the city. The cafe serves coffee, tea, sandwiches, pastries, and other healthy goodies. For leisurely browsing, tables and chairs are set up on both the main level and mezzanine.

All Bookstore Cafe profits go to Housing Works, the parent organization dedicated to "a healing community of people living with and affected by HIV/AIDS." Their volunteer thrift shops around the city fund its mission to "end the dual crises of homelessness and AIDS through relentless advocacy, lifesaving services, and entrepreneurial businesses." Tirelessly fighting for the dignity of all marginalized people, including drug users and sexual minorities, this grassroots organization is committed to the use of nonviolent civil disobedience to advance its agenda.

To achieve these ends, Housing Works Bookstore Cafe hosts a full schedule of special events geared to continuously raise the consciousness of the community at large. Monthly events include lectures, seminars, classes, and discussions on a wide range of topics from a wide range of talents – readings by both famous and upcoming authors, book signings, open Q&A's, writing workshops, networking techniques, talks on travel, cooking, and a great deal more cultural feed.

Get comfortable here, where the aroma of fresh-brewed coffee mingles with funky background music. It's not a stretch to say you will feel very much at home in the Bookstore Cafe.

Address 126 Crosby Street (near Houston Street), New York 10012, Phone
+1 212.334.3324, www.housingworks.org, info@housingworks.org | Transit Subway:
Broadway–Lafayette (B, D, F, M); Bleecker St (6); Prince St (N, R), Bus: M5, M21, M103 |
Hours Mon–Fri 10am–9pm, Sat–Sun 10am–5pm

47 Jacques Torres Chocolate
How sweet it is ...

Affectionately known as Mr. Chocolate, Jacques Torres is proud of his exquisite creations, all handmade with premium ingredients – from marzipan and marshmallows to peanut butter and cookie dough. Each confection is a celebration of chocolate at its purest, never containing preservatives, additives, or extracts. Called "New York's own Willy Wonka," Torres entices us with a mouth-watering repertoire of chocolate bars, bon-bons, ice creams, drink concotions, and an assortment of goodies like buttery caramels, nutty pralines, pure and simple ganaches, exotic tea and spice infusions, and chocolate blended with real fruit and wine. Each of the five retail shops in the city offers an entire menu of confections, including the inimitable, thick, rich hot chocolate – not to be missed – and also served frozen!

It was the ultimate dream of master pastry chef Torres to create a chocolate wonderland and become one of the first artisans in the US to produce the lovely little treasures from scratch, starting with natural cocoa beans. When his establishment first opened in 2000 in the industrial waterfront area of Brooklyn known as Dumbo, it was a fledgling residential neighborhood, not yet widely known. Torres and his business partner designed and built the space one phase at a time. It started as a wholesale factory, designed to supply other outlets with chocolate products. But the workshop, where the velvety chocolate was prepared, proved so popular that people thronged to the glass-enclosed facility to watch the process and buy freshly made sweets.

Owing to the success of the business, the factory section has since moved to another location to make room for the endless stream of customers clamoring for the best chocolate in New York. The workshop/factory has now morphed into a retail boutique-cafe, so you can indulge in your most decadent chocolate fantasy.

Address 66 Water Street (near Main Street), Brooklyn 11201, Phone +1 718.875.1269, www.mrchocolate.com, info@mrchocolate.com | Transit Subway: High St (A,C); York St (F), Bus: B 25, B 67, B 69 | Hours Mon–Sat 9am–8pm, Sun 10am–6pm

48_ J.J. Hat Center

Where 'old hat' is the new cool

The golden days of the Easter Parade along Fifth Avenue – when fashionable New Yorkers strutted their stuff to flaunt fancy hats – have faded into memory. J. J. Hats, founded in 1911, was one among many high-fashion shops and elegant department stores along that route. This venerable establishment is still an old-fashioned haberdashery, providing visitors with a trip through millinery history. As you enter, you're drawn back in time to when most men wore hats about town. Think 1950s, when fedoras were standard fare in the male wardrobe for both dressy and sporty attire. In early twentieth century they wore top hats, bowlers, and boaters. The good news now is that traditional styles are totally hip, reflected in the latest fashions.

J.J.'s is New York's oldest and largest hat store, with over 10,000 pieces in stock. Primarily for gentlemen, the shop also carries a creative line of toppers for the ladies. If you're in the market for that special hat, you've come to the right place. The staff will gently guide you to a selection, but they're never pushy.

Here are a few tips from the experts: To get the best value, choose a hat you can dress up or dress down. A wide brim might overwhelm a slim or short frame, while a small brim may be too dainty. Turn up the brim for a casual look – a style popular with Europeans and musicians. To go dressier, snap the brim down. To be more formal, don a fur felt derby, classy homburg, or even a top hat. The derby is the most popular of the trio since it can easily transition from dressy to casual. For an elegant look in summer, try a Panama hat with a golf shirt, a white button-down, or a khaki suit. Most important is versatility – find a style to go with various outfits on a variety of occasions.

For fun, check out the hats signed by celebrities. Then go ahead, try on some authentic toppers with old-style memories – it will make you feel civilized.

Address 310 Fifth Avenue (near 32nd Street), New York 10001, Phone +1 212.239.4368, www.porkpiehatters.com, jjhatctr@aol.com | Transit Subway: 34 St-Herald Sq (B, D, F, M, N, Q, R); 33 St (6), Bus: M1, M2, M3, M4, M5, M7, M34 | Hours Mon–Fri 9am–6pm, Sat 9:30am–5:30pm

49 John Derian Company

Not just a pretty picture

With the hip New Museum, hot Bowery Hotel, trendy clubs, and chic boutiques nearby, this shop is in one of the city's most dramatically reincarnated neighborhoods – sporting high style, high culture, and high rents. Along with the area, John Derian evolved from creative East Village artist to successful entrepreneur.

His three adjacent storefronts on Second Street have a rustic feel. Weathered wood and barn tools surround finely crafted goods to furnish a home, fashion an apartment, or give as fanciful gifts. All three are John Derian Company, each with its own specialty: furniture; dry goods; home accessories with decoupage at its core. And the whimsical assortment of decoupage wares is a visual feast!

Decoupage is an age-old craft: paper cut-outs lacquered onto various objects transform them into unique decorative items. An artist cuts pictures and shapes to create a design or collage before applying several layers of glue to a jewelry box, photo album, frame, or almost anything. It can elevate the everyday to the exceptional – the possibilities are endless.

Derian was always an avid collector of paper ephemera – old prints, postcards, labels, letters, newsprint. "Images talk to me, they connect to deep feelings," says John, who began using his lovely scraps to make decoupage 25 years ago. The pieces struck a chord in the marketplace and his business took off. Now a team of trained artisans creates them in his East Village studio. Using a colorful arsenal of antique imagery meant to make you smile, reminisce, yearn, or simply admire, they produce all kinds of hand-blown glassware: platters and trays, coasters and cake pedestals, pencil cups, lightswitch covers, lamps, and wall art.

Come in and find the pictorial message that speaks to you: a giant-eyeball clock *(here's looking at you)*, or a clipper-ship coin dish *(come away with me)*, or a single precious word on a paperweight *(love)*.

Address 6 East 2nd Street (near Bowery), New York 10003, Phone +1 212.677.3917, www.johnderian.com, shop@johnderian.com | Transit Subway: 2nd Ave (F); Bleecker St (6); Broadway-Lafayette (B, D, M), Bus: M 5, M 15, M 21, M 103 | Hours Tue–Sun 12–7pm, closed Sun in August

50 Juicy Lucy
Drink to your health!

Sometimes a place is defined by its space. This nifty little juice joint at the corner of 1st Avenue & 1st Street is a wooden shack with a footprint of only 45 square feet, and it's become a beloved local landmark.

Since 1996, in all kinds of weather, it has served East Villagers (and lucky passersby) delicious fresh-squeezed juices and smoothies, soul-warming hot soups and cider on frigid days, the neighborhood's favorite *café con leche*, and healthful concoctions to heal what ails you, like a wheatgrass shot or the Energy Boost, Cold Helper, or morning-after Hangover Cure.

It was one of the very first juice bars in an area now littered with them. Many say it's still the best. Most popular are the acai drinks and bowls, mixed with tropical fruits and berries. A new cold-press extraction method uses just enough pressure while preserving nutrients and flavor better than traditional juicers.

René Henricks was tending bar at a restaurant on that corner when an opportunity to do her own thing opened up. The tenement building's owner, a free-spirited artist and die-hard East Villager, liked the idea of a small business serving juiced-from-the-fruit libations and fresh-brewed coffees out of his vacant shed.

This ramshackle structure has its own history: built in the late 1800s for storage, it was transformed pre-WWI into a shoeshine shed (a common sight in old New York), then became a florist stand in the flower-power 1970s, and by the 1990s it was sitting empty just waiting for a fresh start. So they hooked up running water and electricity, and Juicy Lucy was an instant hit in what was then a heavily ethnic neighborhood peppered with artists and musicians. René's background is Cuban, so the stand has a Latino flavor. Even though the area's recent makeover has made it more upscale, René maintains high quality while prices remain affordable.

As one of Juicy Lucy's devoted employees says, "This is juice for the people."

Address 72 East 1st Street (at First Avenue), New York 10003, Phone +1 212.777.5829, juicylucy@gogosurfer.com | Transit Subway: 2nd Ave (F), Bus: M 8, M 9, M 14A, M 15, M 21, M 103 | Hours Daily 7am–7pm

51 Kalustyan's

New York's global pantry

Beneath the bright, colorful awning at the entrance of Kalustyan's is New York's oldest, largest exotic spices and specialty food market, located in the eastside neighborhood of Little India. At first you're overwhelmed by the sharp sweet perfume of spice, then by row upon row of over 4,000 different imported foods, meticulously organized on three levels.

Turkish-Armenian Kalustyan opened an Indian spice and grocery shop in 1944. Today this veritable cornucopia of global ingredients and flavors carries a staggering variety of nearly every edible: vinegars, sauces, rices, noodles, grains, lentils, nuts, dried fruits, olives, candies, breads, mustards, honeys, pickles, chutneys, oils, and cheeses. Walls are stacked high with different salts, sugars and chili peppers. There are also hundreds of teas, beans, condiments. While the emphasis is on Indian, Persian, Turkish, and other Middle Eastern items, nearly every country on the planet is represented – a United Nations for foodies. You can find foods from Australia, Africa, South America, Asia, Europe – every corner of the world.

It's hard to exercise self-control in here. Maybe you can limit yourself to a recipe's ingredients, but more likely you'll toss lots of gotta-have-thats into your basket. Every kind of cook shops here, from curious beginner to experienced experimenter to professional chef. That's because they can find virtually everything they need. There's even an entire section on molecular cuisine, a new culinary twist that takes advantage of technical innovations in food science.

Besides a dizzying abundance of the hard-to-find and unexpected, Kalustyan's has another surprise: a Middle Eastern deli tucked away upstairs with just a few tables, offering fresh platters, sandwiches, and soup for those lucky enough (mostly locals and wandering customers) to discover the hidden eatery. Stop by to browse, shop, or for a snack. Even if you don't love to cook, everyone loves to eat.

Address 123 Lexington Avenue (near 28th Street), New York 10016, Phone +1 212.685.3451, www.kalustyans.com, sales@kalustyans.com | Transit Subway: 28 St (6, N, R), Bus: M 1, M 2, M 3, M 5, M 9, M 15, M 23, M 34, M 102, M 103 | Hours Mon–Sat 10am–8pm, Sun 11am–7pm

52 Kiki de Montparnasse

Sassy and classy

Borrowing its name from the famous Parisian artists' mecca and nightlife district, this erotic Soho boutique is a sophisticated environment dedicated entirely to the fantasized romantic sexual experience. Its dusky purple interior invokes images of swanky private French salons. Tastefully decadent photographs and art dot the landscape, mingling with seductive apparel and pricey sex paraphernalia. Kiki's exclusive limited edition and handmade items, elegant lingerie, erotic jewelry, and intimate toys complement sophisticated home decor, art, and books – all intended to create an immersive environment to engage all the senses. A select apothecary of sultry bath and body products laced with aphrodisiac ingredients stimulate the erotic imagination and set a new standard for indulgent self-pampering.

And of course there are the intriguing 'sexessories' – masks and blindfolds, belts and gloves, and an array of instruments of pleasure luxuriously crafted from the highest quality materials, including the Restraining Arts Kit, priced at over $1,000. No question, this is a luxury sex shop.

The lovely intimate apparel, made of fine silks, cashmeres, leathers, and velvets, is designed to appeal to a wide range of tastes, settings, and moods, from coquette to concubine. And these provocative styles may venture beyond the boudoir, perhaps even flaunted in public at a special event, raising an eyebrow or two.

Kiki's philosophy is that sensual pleasure is an essential part of the good life; intimacy should be honored and honorable; and lovers should be able to express their passion with both grace and abandon. The ultimate goal of Kiki de Montparnasse is to bathe you in the warm stream of sensuality, to get your psyche to accept the transformative power of erotic license, and to hook you into the uninhibited expression of love. This experience can be both intoxicating and addictive. But what a way to go!

Address 79 Greene Street (near Spring Street), New York 10012, Phone +1 212.965.8150, www.kikidm.com, info@kikidm.com | **Transit** Subway: Prince St (N, R); Spring St (6, C, E); Canal St (Q); Lafayette St (B, D, F, M), Bus: M 5, M 20, M 21 | **Hours** Sun – Mon 11am – 7pm, Tue – Sat 11am – 8pm

53 Kossar's Bialys

The authentic undisputed roll with a dimple

While the great bagel boom has infiltrated the western world with mass-produced rings of boiled dough, New York has managed to preserve one of its secret baking recipes – the bialy, a taste treat considered to be cousin to the bagel. Originating from Bialystok, Poland, these traditional *kuchen* – made of a yeasted dough smeared with a garlic-onion paste – are baked in a brick oven, yielding a tender roll with a crisp outer crust and a hand-indented well in the center for the paste.

The best of this singular treat undeniably comes from Kossar's Bakery, where you can still buy an oven-hot bialy for under a dollar. Purists insist that their short shelf life won't pass the taste test on the following day, which is why bialys have been called the "gypsy moths of the baking world." (Nevertheless, toasting day-old bialys restores much of their original flavor and texture.) Protocol calls not for slicing it open, but for spreading butter or cream cheese either over the top or on the bottom of the roll, taking care not to shake loose the precious bits of onion along the way.

Kossar's opened in 1935 and is still in the heart of the Lower East Side. It has changed hands from the original family a few times and now enthusiastic new owners are making traditional bialys, and have added bagels too. Here you can watch the bakers work the bialy dough, dimple it and fill it, then pull the hot *kuchen* out of the giant brick oven, even as you place your order.

Bialys contain love and history – a reminder of the security of home and family from the old days. When restaurant critic Mimi Sheraton was writing her book *The Bialy Eaters: The Story of a Bread and a Lost World*, she interviewed an elderly Bialystoker. He was perplexed that she planned to travel to his hometown in Poland to research the secrets of the bialy. "Why go so far?" he asked. "Kossar's is only two blocks away. Delicious *kuchen!*"

Address 367 Grand Street (near Essex Street), New York 10002, Phone +1 212.473.4810, www.kossarsbialys.com, info@kossarsbialys.com | Transit Subway: Delancey St (F); Essex St (J, M, Z), Bus: M 9, M 14A, M 15, M 22 | Hours Mon–Thurs 6am–7pm, Fri 6am–3pm, Sat 10pm–Sun 7pm

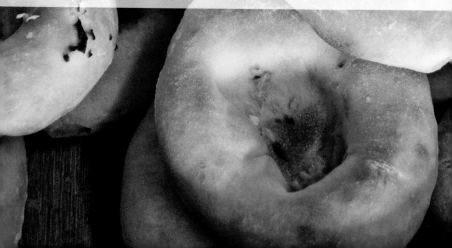

54 Laina Jane

From bustiers to booties

Women are complicated, beautiful creatures. They play many roles, often at the same time. A woman who feels like a sexy seductive siren may very well also be a naturally nurturing mother. And except for full-service department stores that cater separately to these distinct female personas – usually a trek away from each other and on different floors – there's only one shop we know of that acknowledges and simultaneously serves both aspects of a woman's psyche: the temptress and the mom.

With the charm of a quaint nook in the heart of the West Village, Laina Jane at first carried everything from girdles to garters, cotton undies to barely-there thongs. Then, what was once a demure little lingerie store on Christopher Street evolved into this one-stop shop for sexy mamas. They had been in business since 1988 and as their loyal clientele changed, so did they. Their single-gal customers began to get married and have babies. These ladies needed bridal wear, then nursing bras, then kiddie clothes. "We adapted," says Lim, one of the three sister-owners of Laina Jane (which has another location uptown that carries only lingerie).

So there's "the sexy window and the baby window," displaying the latest styles, for both the daring and the darling, depending on whom you're buying for. Their well-curated selection is not run-of-the-mill. Find both unique designer lingerie and imported, hard-to-find infantwear. And think about great shower gifts – whether bridal or baby shower, you've got it covered! Lovely, lacy, edgy. Sweet, cuddly, adorable. Affordable and exceptional – it's all here.

Celebrating the true beauty of a woman's figure, Laina Jane understands how a properly fitted undergarment can transform her appearance and attitude. Expert bra-fitting is a specialty – customers call Lim the bra-whisperer. "I know your size just by looking." In my case, even wearing a down parka, she was spot on.

Address 45 Christopher Street (near Seventh Avenue), New York 10014, Phone +1 212.807.8077, www.lainajane.com | Transit Subway: Christopher St-Sheridan Sq (1); West 4 St (A, B, C, D, E, F, M), Bus: M 5, M 8, M 20 | Hours Daily 11:30am–7:30pm

55 __ Laura Lobdell

Jewelry with a champagne punch

It's no stretch to say this is NYC's greatest *little* shop. The lilliputian space (a shoebox store measuring a mere 4x16 feet) holds a very small crowd – barely room for more than two visitors at a time. But when you see the understated, textured, and whimsical found-object jewelry so artfully and effectively displayed, you realize that, in fact, size doesn't matter.

Owner and artist Laura Lobdell is a champagne Cinderella in a fairytale setting – a golden-haired, sparkly-eyed, fair maiden. She welcomes you into her intimate world of art. A hand-wrought chandelier of glitter-tinged champagne corks enveloped in a cloud of pink tulle hovers beneath a silver pressed-tin ceiling. Laura's aristocratic companion, a Japanese Chin lapdog, is an integral part of the shop's ambience and personality – its theme is *Celebrate Every Day*.

Then there's the jewelry. It's not easy to achieve uniqueness in a field brimming with the brilliant imaginings of today's contemporary jewelry designers. But Laura has created her own niche in this competitive world, and you may not find anything else quite as inventive in your travels.

Like the Guitar Pick: originally made for her musician friends, the hand-sculpted sterling silver pick threaded with leather is destined to be strung around the neck. Or magical Bubbles Royale: a classic bubble wand of silver or gold (complete with liquid bubbles, of course). In Seeds of Silk she hand-knots strands of ocean-washed silk in subtle natural colors to create fabric bracelets and necklaces embedded with pearls, stones, and silver bits. Or the Longitude & Gratitude surf bracelets: wide silk bands printed with the map coordinates of world-class sailing destinations and clasped with a polished cowrie shell for good fortune. These friendship bracelets are "best worn when piled on a wrist full of memories." Let's have a toast to the work of a witty and romantic artist!

Address 183⅛ West 10th Street (near Seventh Avenue), New York 10014, **Phone** +1 646.272.8483, www.lauralobdell.com, info@lauralobdell.com | **Transit** Subway: Christopher St-Sheridan Sq (1); West 4 St (A, B, C, D, E, F, M); 14 St-6 Ave (2, 3), Bus: M 5, M 8, M 14, M 20 | **Hours** Mon–Sat 1–7pm, call to confirm summer hours

56 __ Let There Be Neon

It's a gas!

This first-of-its-kind gallery was the brainchild of psychedelic-light artist Rudi Stern, who in 1972 envisioned a brighter future for a then-floundering medium. Not only did he see continued commercial use for neon signage, but this enlightened guru created an appreciation for its unique esthetic. The original studio was part of a booming new art scene in Soho – where Stern attracted an unlikely mix of artists, craftspeople, fabricators, and philosophers – merging diverse components to create something fresh and vital: neon as art.

Developed by a Frenchman, neon made its first major public appearance in Paris in 1910 in two 38-foot-long glass tubes. In 1923 a Los Angeles Packard car dealership had the first sign in the US, and by the 1930s flashy neons flickered all across the country. Within a few more years Times Square was all lit up!

Today, LTBN is a bustling gallery/studio/workshop in Tribeca making signs for storefronts, window displays, restaurants, trendy retro shops, and for film and TV productions (like *Sex and the City*). LTBN's stable of contemporary artists creates custom works for individual clients and their homes. And there's a new niche market: 'love neon' for wedding receptions – because nothing says LOVE like neon.

Signs are made in the back of the studio by glass-benders who start with straight glass 'sticks,' twist them into the desired shapes, fill them with gas, add a spark, and presto!

Visitors are welcome to come in and browse the gallery's ever-changing display of vintage and current commissioned pieces awaiting pick-up. Some displays are available for purchase, as are cool Let There Be Neon t-shirts, and Rudi's revised classic book, *The New Let There Be Neon*. Depending on how busy they are, the staff can be extremely helpful, or just cheerfully direct you to the nearest tavern for some refreshment.

Neon gas may be inert, but neon art is all a-buzz!

Address 38 White Street (near Church Street), New York 10013, Phone +1 212.226.4883, www.lettherebeneon.com, info@lettherebeneon.com | Transit Subway: Canal St (A, C, E); Franklin St (1); Canal St (6, J, M, Z, N, Q, R), Bus: M 5, M 9, M 20, M 22 | Hours Mon–Fri 9am–5pm

57__The Little Lebowski Shop

Where a movie becomes a store

This is one of those quaint little shops that characterize old Greenwich Village. Not much bigger than a school bus in size, it would be easily overlooked if not for the life-size cutout of The Dude standing out front during store hours.

Yes, The Dude. The character immortalized by actor Jeff Bridges in the Coen Brothers' quirky 1998 film noir/stoner movie spoof, *The Big Lebowski*, now a cult classic. Far out, man.

Ninety percent of the merchandise in the store is *Lebowski*-themed: t-shirts, mugs, tumblers, and "coozies" (can/bottle insulators) emblazoned with quotes from this endlessly quotable movie – as well as a number of books, action figures, and DVDs of selected Coen Brothers and Jeff Bridges films. They sell t-shirts designed by a local artist who creates images with a mix of scientific, pop culture, and religious themes. One corner of the store is a mock set-up of a bowling alley, the locale where some key scenes of the movie take place.

The store opened in 2007 as a souvenir shop that included nerd culture as well as the usual I♥NY stuff. When reconstruction of nearby Washington Square Park temporarily closed off their street, owners Nick and Preston tried everything to stay alive – morphing into a comic book emporium, then selling pop-culture ephemera.

It turned out that t-shirts were the real winners. When two Big Lebowski-themed shirts entered the mix, those items proved phenomenally popular, outselling all others. Customers spoke of Lebowski-fest and Dudeism, and how popular The Dude is in Italy. "We call him Drugo," said one cool Roman. Adding more Lebowski shirts increased sales dramatically and The Dude virtually took over the store, which reinvented itself as The Little Lebowski Shop.

Nick and Preston, two pop-culture freaks, have managed to make a successful store based on a single movie. To our knowledge, this is the only *Lebowski* shop in the world. And, of course, The Dude abides here.

Address 215 Thompson Street (near Bleecker), New York 10012, Phone +1 212.388.1466, www.littlelebowskishop.com, littlelebowskishop@gmail.com | Transit Subway: West 4 St (A, B, C, D, E, F, M); Houston St (1, 2, 3), Bus: M 5, M 21 | Hours Mon 12–9pm, Tue–Sat 11am–10pm, Sun 12–7pm

58 Lomography Shop

Back to the future?

In 1992, when a group of creative Viennese students stumbled upon the Lomo Kompakt Automat – an enigmatic little Russian camera – they were intrigued by its unique, intensely colorful, often fuzzy, mind-blowing images. This quirky discovery spawned an international Society, a Movement, a Community, and eventually a new line of film cameras designed to intentionally produce radical special effects – oversaturation, extreme optical distortion, over- or under-exposure, blurring – qualities traditionally considered 'bad photography.' Lomography emerged as an anti-digital-camera revolution, favoring analog equipment and processes over the increasingly common and popular hi-tech versions. Today it's an "active organization dedicated to experimental and creative visual expression."

Its philosophy: *Don't think. Just shoot.* Lomography's Golden Rules advise enthusiasts to "be prepared to throw all inhibitions about photography to the wind." Some hints: Be spontaneous, use odd angles, shoot anywhere at any time. Minimize formal and traditional practices, shoot from the hip (literally). Be fast. Don't preconceive your photo. And… don't worry about rules!

Lomography maintains a strong community following on the internet, encouraging free sharing of images and techniques. The Society encourages social activism and has worked with Light of the World raising money for vision care in Kenya, and the International Red Cross for famine relief in East Africa.

The Greenwich Village shop is a feast for the eyes – a candy-colored assortment of cameras on display to pick up and try out. Their on-site photo lab develops film and processes printing. Its knock-out LomoWall, a 3-story skylight atrium room papered by thousands of NYC images submitted by lomographers everywhere, bears the motto *The Future Is Analog.* You'll be awestruck by what the past has futuristically brought very much into the present!

Address 41 West 8th Street (near Sixth Avenue), New York 10011, Phone +1 212.529.4353, www.lomography.com, shopnyc@lomography.com | Transit Subway: West 4 St (A, B, C, D, E, F, M); Christopher St-Sheridan Sq (1); 8 St-NYU (N, R); Astor Pl (6), Bus: M 1, M 3, M 5, M 8 | Hours Mon–Sat 11am–8pm, Sun 11am–7pm

59 Love Adorned

Charmed, I'm sure

The new personality of this old Bowery neighborhood has an almost magical quality, impressively transformed from the once-sordid streets littered with winos and panhandlers. Now the area known as Nolita attracts a hip upscale crowd to its chic restaurants and fanciful boutiques, like the lovely gem of a shop Love Adorned.

Lured by the curvaceous neon sign and colorful goodies glimpsed through the glass front wall, hear your own oohs and aahs as you drift in from the street. Meander through the spacious shop, admire the diversity of artfully displayed baubles and treasures. The selection of unusual items aims to give pleasure and ease to our complicated lives, to make the body cleaner, the mind clearer. Distancing itself from America's throwaway consumer culture, Love Adorned strives to make a difference with durable goods of lasting value. This lifestyle-concept store offers smart tools for home, body, and travel.

In perpetual search of original design and fine craftsmanship, owner Lori Leven sees her choices as potential milestones in our lives, highlighting eclectic, sometimes obscure, wares and remedies. Leven's passion for global travel has led her to scores of artisans on six continents. Discover a beguiling assortment of designer, vintage, and antique jewelry crafted of everything from pebbles to diamonds, homespun garments and textiles, useful travel accessories, pottery, perfume, unique kids' stuff, and a select apothecary. Browse Brazilian crystals, African tribal fabrics, Afghan beaded door hangings, cypress wood bath mats, and Pakistani rosewood mortar & pestles; or unique items like a Navajo tribal buffalo pin and a Victorian vinaigrette box.

Since its opening in 2011, Love Adorned has become a destination for those who seek exceptional objects. Whether looking to treat yourself or find a gift to be cherished, this sparkling store will inspire you with its varied choices and stylish taste.

Address 269 Elizabeth Street (near Houston Street), New York 10012, Phone +1 212.431.5683, www.loveadorned.com, love@loveadorned.com | **Transit** Subway: Bleecker St (6); Broadway-Lafayette (B, D, F, M), Bus: M 15, M 21, M 103 | **Hours** Daily 12–8pm

60 Manhattan Art & Antiques Center

One of New York's better kept secrets

There's the famous Paris Flea Market. London's got its meandering Portobello Road Street Market. Istanbul has its historic labyrinthine Bazaar. On a smaller scale, but just as varied and layered, is New York's own Manhattan Art & Antiques Center, located right in midtown. A must visit for serious collectors, architects, designers, and antiques buffs, MAAC is also the perfect destination for anyone hunting down that special gift – or just for curious browsing of the myriad items displayed in its more than one hundred galleries.

Extraordinary treasures of all descriptions reside within these shops, which occupy a building dedicated entirely to antiquities. Connected by a wide central spiral staircase, the galleries are laid out on three spacious floors – overflowing with marvelous European, Asian, American, and African artifacts and artwork. This multifarious reliquary is a real discovery!

For more than forty years MAAC has established itself as the city's oldest emporium for a dizzying selection of period furniture, silver, porcelain, jewelry, tapestries, rugs, clocks, paintings, sculpture, bronzes, books, lighting, glassware, chinaware, statuary – collectibles from all eras, in all styles. With the welcoming, elegant ambience of an international hotel shopping concourse, each gallery is more intriguing than the last. There's so much to wonder at, admire, and covet that even if you're not in the market to buy, walking through and chatting with the sometimes eccentric dealers is an engaging treat.

Manhattan Art & Antiques Center is one of the city's great hidden-in-plain-sight gems. From the odd spoon to the museum-quality urn, there are so many choices you won't know where to begin. So pack a snack and spend the entire day treasure-hunting in midtown. Savor the rare and beautiful, the glittering and strange, the exotic and puzzling – things you've never seen before or perhaps even knew existed.

Address 1050 Second Avenue (near 55th Street), New York 10022, Phone
+1 212.355.4400, www.the-maac.com, info@the-maac.com | Transit Subway: Lexington
Ave-53 St (E, M); 59 St-Lexington Ave (4, 5, 6, N, Q, R), Bus: M 15, M 31, M 50, M 57,
M 102, M 103 | Hours Mon–Sat 10:30am–6pm, Sun 12–6pm

61__Manhattan Kayak Company

A real "trip" for a sunny day!

As you walk through the wide-open portal, you're struck by the vibrant colors of floor-to-ceiling stacks of kayaks and paddleboards. Then you break out onto a sun-filled dock that slopes right onto the river. You're surrounded by rows of colorful life vests hanging out to dry in the sun.

Not exactly a store, Manhattan Kayak is more of an experience: kayak and paddleboard lessons and tours on the great and historic Hudson River. It's an opportunity to feel the ebb and flow of this busy waterway, with its endless parade of ferries, tugboats, barges, sailing yachts, partying cruise ships – and a broadside view of the USS Intrepid. Dramatic cityscape views of the skyline and harbor are unforgettable from water level.

The young staff are all experienced professionals. They offer instruction and tours for people of all ages and abilities. Fitted with life vests and paddles on dry land, beginners are expertly drilled in the basics of kayaking or paddleboarding before heading down to the water. Then, sitting in a kayak or kneeling on a paddleboard, you practice your first strokes in relatively calm waters around the dock before venturing out further. Depending on weather conditons and the level of your group – from novice to expert – the experience can be mildy adventurous or action-packed and challenging. But absolutely indelible.

MKC's boutique also sells everything from kayaks and paddleboards to life vests, wet suits, watersport clothes, t-shirts, hats, and other paraphernalia.

We tried the paddleboard our first time out. Shaky at first, we gained confidence during the hour-long lesson – which was fun, challenging, and ultimately exhilerating. At the end, as we stepped onto the dock, one sassy instructor with a big grin looked at my partner Susan and remarked, "You're all dry." Then, looking at me, he said: "And you are *all wet*. Now, how did *that* happen!?"

Address 555 Twelfth Avenue (Pier 84 at West 44th Street), New York 10036, Phone
+1 212.924.1788, www.manhattankayak.com, info@manhattankayak.com | Transit Subway:
42 St-Port Authority (A, C, E), Bus: M 11, M 42, M 50 | Hours Mon–Fri 12–9pm,
Sat–Sun 9am–9pm (hours vary with daylight)

62 __ Manhattan Saddlery

Where you hold the reins

As New York's only remaining tack shop, Manhattan Saddlery carries on a long tradition of catering to the equestrian's needs – whether you take lessons, actively compete, or ride simply for pleasure. Specializing in English-style riding, the Saddlery features not only equipment, but also a fashionable array of riding clothes from cap to boot, whether for show or barn wear.

In 1912, a Russian master harness-maker opened the shop in a neighborhood lined with stables and carriage houses. Horse-drawn carts and carriages were the major players in the city's transportation infrastructure. The original family business, Miller's, was built into a veritable empire that the *New York Times* described as "the equine epicenter of New York," patronized by well-heeled notables like the Rockefellers and the Kennedys. Their reputation for expert, hands-on service became almost legendary. A customer was once invited to lead her horse onto the store's freight elevator so the staff could give her the best possible consultation on the fit of a harness part.

Over the years, as the horseless carriage replaced the horse, demand for riding equipment waned. The number of stables in Manhattan diminished, then disappeared, and the store was in imminent danger of folding. When new owners took over in 2002, renaming it Manhattan Saddlery, they reached out to a broader market by focusing on a more inclusive price-range and appealing to all levels of equestrian skill. Riding stables and academies in the outer boroughs and nearby suburban areas now attract Manhattan equestrians.

Whether you are new to riding, compete at the Olympic level, or just love the equestrian lifestyle, everything is here: the store's main level will outfit you in elegant, classic style, and the lower level can do the same for your horse. Manhattan Saddlery will put you in the saddle – whether in reality or in your rich imagination.

Address 117 East 24th Street (near Park Avenue), New York 10010, Phone +1 212.673.1400, www.manhattansaddlery.com, info@manhattansaddlery.com | Transit Subway: 23 St (6, N, R), Bus: M1, M3, M23, M102, M103 | Hours Mon–Sat 10am–7pm

63 Martinez Hand-Rolled Cigars

Sometimes a cigar is not just a cigar

If you're not struck by the aroma of fresh tobacco leaves wafting out to the street, once you enter this cozy den of a store you may be overwhelmed by the thick, rich odor of cigar smoke. It's not just from customers puffing away, relaxing in well-worn comfy chairs, but permanently embedded in the woodwork since 1974. NY sports heroes' autographs and memorabilia proudly grace the walls. This old-time cigar factory is really a neighborhood meeting place where regulars, locals, workers, curious passersby, and aficionados democratically come together to share a good story and a great cigar.

At the rolling tables nestled into one corner of the store sit a few highly skilled workers, the *tabaqueros*, expertly selecting and blending cured tobacco leaves (filler) surrounded by softer leaves (binders) and finishing off with an outer layer (wrapper). Rolled fresh every day, the end product is a handmade premium cigar, in sizes ranging from slim cigarillo to inch-thick full-bodied classic. There are dozens of blends and styles to choose from, with colorful names like *bandito, corona, pasión, robusto,* and *torpedo.* Tobaccos are carefully chosen and purchased in bales by owner Jesus Martinez, who travels the world in search of the finest leaves from plantations in Honduras, Nicaragua, Ecuador, Dominican Republic, Brazil, Cameroon, and Sumatra. (Cuba is not yet on the itinerary.)

We all associate cigars with congratulations on special occasions: a new baby, wedding, promotion, or retirement. "Have a cigar!" means there's something big to celebrate. Martinez specializes in creating custom cigar bands for any occasion.

At Martinez, cigars are a lifestyle. A perfect puff awaits anyone who loves the taste, feel, and aroma of this hallowed smoking tradition. The friendly, clubby atmosphere is welcoming and filled with lively conversation. And most of all, Martinez offers camaraderie on a walk-in basis.

Address 171 West 29th Street (near Seventh Avenue), New York 10001, Phone +1 212.239.4049, www.martinezcigars.com, sales@martinezcigars.com | Transit Subway: 28 St (1, N, R); 34 St-Penn St (2, 3, A, C, E); 34 St-Herald Sq (D, F, Q), Bus: M 1, M 3, M 4, M 5, M 7, M 20, M 34 | Hours Mon–Fri 7am–7pm, Sat 10am–6pm

64_Metropolitan Museum Store

Museum-quality shopping

For more than a century the Met has offered top-quality reproductions to satisfy the urge to *possess* something that touches us deeply. A souvenir can refresh that sensation of the original's beauty and power.

A visit to this primo destination along Fifth Avenue's Museum Mile, with its immense storehouse of world-class art and history, can be overwhelming. Seeing even a small portion of its vast reserves, your head swims with impressions. You feel both inspired and exhausted. To unwind, wander through the main gift shop – it's like an instant replay of museum highlights, except here, you can touch! The space is brimming with collection-based reproductions and inspirations: exquisite jewelry spanning the ages; deliciously patterned silk ties and scarves; iconic sculptures and *objets*; lavish art books, all eras and styles; current and past exhibit catalogs; toys, crafts, and gifts for kids of all ages – like a pop-up dollhouse of period rooms at the Met, or a Lego set of a Frank Lloyd Wright house. Expect the unexpected.

But here's the big secret: most visitors are unaware that the Met also sells *original art*, not just replicas. A little-known gallery in the world's greatest museum offers original prints and textiles selected by the savviest art buyers in the world. The shop's mezzanine level displays signed limited edition prints, ceramics, and photographs by a virtual *Who's Who* of modern artists, such as Rauschenberg, Christo, Indiana. Prices go from modest to mega – a recent David Hockney sold for fifteen large. And there are magnificent artisanal rugs: the shop's buyer travels to Turkey to handpick one-of-a-kind kilims, tribal textiles, and nomadic pieces in both contemporary and traditional patterns. Brilliantly colored hand-dyed silk and wool pieces are offered here from regions all over the Middle East.

Come home from your trip to the museum not just as a spectator, but as an art collector!

Address The Metropolitan Museum of Art, 1000 Fifth Avenue, New York 10028,
Phone +1 212.570.3894, www.store.metmuseum.org, customer.service@metmuseum.org |
Transit Subway: 86 St (1, 4, 5, 6), 81 St (C); Bus: M1, M2, M3, M4, M79, M86 |
Hours Sun–Thurs 10am–5.15pm, Fri–Sat 10am–8.45pm

65 Moishe's Bake Shop

A taste of the Old World

Described as a shop that "hasn't changed since forever," this East Village Jewish bakery, located in the heart of what was once the Yiddish Theater District, is a 1970s-vintage mainstay for authentic kosher baking that your grandma loved, and you will too. Moishe's is the Promised Land for anyone craving classic *babka, rugelach, challah, mandelbrot,* black-and-white cookies, seven-layer cake (by the pound), and old-world breads like pumpernickel rye. Glass display cases are packed with a jewel-like assortment of tantalizing pastries. Some are specially featured for traditional holidays, like *taiglach* for Rosh Hashana, *sufganiyot* for Chanukah, and *hamentaschen* for Purim (but available here year-round). Moishe's makes some of New York's best ethnic pastries and has often been cited as one of the city's top kosher bakeries.

The owner, Moishe Perlmutter, came to America from Germany after World War II. His father was a baker who taught Moishe everything there was to know about authentic Jewish recipes. By 1972, when the business first opened, that lower portion of Second Avenue was seedy-looking, but rents were affordable in a neighborhood that was predominantly Polish, Ukranian, and Jewish. Moishe started what came to be regarded not just as a neighborhood staple, but an East Village institution.

In recent years, because the ethnic mix of the neighborhood has changed, this local shop gets as crowded on Easter as on Passover. The graffitied storefront, ravaged by time and vandals of yesteryear, is a testament to its longevity. Perhaps its popularity is due to Moishe's warm spirit and commanding presence, with his long beard and folksy yiddish accent. Or the almost tacky interior that harks back to mid-twentieth century. Or simply the quality of the goods. Whatever its appeal, this cherished relic of the past makes an excellent argument for the future preservation of the old East Village.

Address 115 Second Avenue (near 7th Street), New York 10003, Phone +1 212.505.8555, www.moishesbakeshop.com | Transit Subway: Astor Pl (6), Bus: M 8, M 15, M 101, M 102, M 103 | Hours Sun–Thurs 7am–9pm, Fri 7am–an hour before sundown, closed Sat

66___Mood Fabrics

Where Miss Universe shops

The day we were there, a dark-haired beauty queen and her dress designer were unfurling long bolts of diaphanous silks and discussing the Miss Universe pageant they were prepping for. The designer held a sparkly sheer chiffon up to her client's face. "This violet is magic for your complexion." It was true – the contestant glowed.

Shopping alongside ambitious home-sewers and savvy DIYer's are famous *haute couture* and ready-to-wear designers, theatrical costumers, stylists, film producers, runway models, and fashion school students. On the three floors of this bustling emporium is everything you need to create, accessorize, or repair whatever can possibly be made of any kind of fabric – natural, synthetic, blend, or faux. It's easy to be overwhelmed by the gargantuan array of prints, velvets, brocades, suiting, leathers, upholstery, walls of buttons, aisles of trimmings, zippers, notions – but it's all well-organized, clearly labeled, and the expert staff is happy to guide and advise you.

In the 1970s, Jack Sauma, a Syrian designer with an American dream, sold his first designs to Swedish mega-chain H&M, then unknown in the US. Moving to New York, he began sewing for famous designers, then started his own clothing line. But he found it more lucrative to sell his beautiful fabrics – wholesale at first, then retail – opening an enormous store upstairs in a garment center office building. When the popular reality TV phenom *Project Runway* showed contestants scouring the aisles of Mood Fabrics for materials to concoct wildly imaginative creations, the store instantly became a must-see destination for fashionistas around the world. Jack's sons now run the store, in the company of Swatch, their now-famous Boston terrier who may be "the most petted dog in the US" – because Mood has 1,200 customers a day!

Advice from one deliriously happy regular: "Bring a snack. You'll be there awhile."

Address 225 West 37th Street, 3rd floor (near Seventh Avenue), New York 10018, Phone +1 212.730.5003, www.moodfabrics.com | Transit Subway: 34 St-Penn Sta (A); 42 St-Times Sq (N, Q, R, 1, 2, 3, 7); 42 St-Port Authority (C, E); 34 St-Herald Sq (B, D, F, M), Bus: M7, M20, M34, M42, M104 | Hours Mon–Fri 9am–7pm, Sat 10am–4pm

67 __Music Inn

And the band played on …

Lost amidst the bars, sex stores, and smoke shops littering West 4th Street, Music Inn's worn, weathered storefront seems to materialize out of time and space. Locals pass by for years without noticing it. Inside is a stalactite cave of low-hanging stringed instruments of every kind, for music makers of every ilk, competing for each available inch of space. This store IS music – play a note and the hollow bodies surrounding you sing back.

Venture down the creaky wooden staircase to 'the dungeon-chamber' where percussion rules; it's also where repairs are made and new ideas and designs are realized, producing some original, amazing instruments. Like the shop's own creation: the Electric Zarod, the next evolution of Indian classical music.

If you seek musical roots there are antique sarods, Japanese shakuhachis, Persian zarbs, African djembes, Indian tablas and sitars, ukuleles, lutes, lute-kuleles, banjos, banjoleles. Come on in, play a variety of instruments – or just sit and chat awhile. Conversation here is an art form, especially about music. Discover used bargains tucked into every nook and crag. Like honored guests they patiently wait, lovingly tended till their dues are paid, and they leave the shop with a new patron and a renewed future.

When it opened in 1958 as a record store people bought LPs, 45s, and 78s (many still live in a remote corner by the ancient coal stove, craving attention). During the folk era in the Village, guitars were the catch of the day, so the records eventually got crowded out by instruments, reflecting the 1960s cultural explosion of music and art. Now Music Inn is even more unique and valued, since nearly all the other neighborhood music stores – cluttered, dusty and finally out of tune with the times – have disappeared.

If you've ever imagined what it would be like to visit a free museum of music where you can touch everything – well, here's your chance.

Address 169 West 4th Street (near Sixth Avenue), New York 10014, Phone
+1 212.243.5715, www.musicinnonline.com, info@musicinnworldinstruments.com |
Transit Subway: West 4 St (A, B, C, D, E, F, M); Christopher St-Sheridan Sq (1),
Bus: M5, M8, M20, M21 | Hours Mon–Sat 10am–7pm

68__ The New York Shaving Company

The barber of civility

Gentleman's Tonsorial Parlor on quiet, tree-lined Elizabeth Street transports you back to a simpler day when men wore fedoras and got their whiskers trimmed at the corner barbershop. Enter at the familiar striped pole and you've stepped through a time machine into another era – picture Bogart or dapper Edward G. Robinson – a masculine bastion with red brick walls, antique barber chairs, and 1940s music. In here, it's a man's world.

Start a special night on the town with a trip to the New York Shaving Company. Choose from a $30 traditional shave or splurge on the $45 ultimate shave, complete with mini-facial. Settle in to a steamy hot towel, pre-shave oil selected for your skin type, and a skillfully handled straight razor expertly brandished by a gent in a crisp white jacket. If time allows, luxuriate with a stimulating scalp treatment, and your skull will tingle with pleasure as you leave the parlor feeling like a new man.

Most guys today know little about correct care of their stubble, from shaving in the wrong direction to using skin-irritating products. New York Shaving Company educates the bearded gender in proper shaving techniques and good grooming, offering free consultation and encouraging use of natural products like rosewater and orange-blossom tonics. The shop carries its own line of products including badger-hair shaving brushes, both straight and safety razors, and various male toiletries. Their locally crafted, all-natural preparations nourish without irritating the skin. In addition to shaves, the parlor offers haircuts, head shaves, beard and mustache trims, and spa-style facials. A shaving kit or gift certificate for the man in your life makes a practical yet elegant gift.

Owner John Scala founded his shop with a simple intention: to reintroduce the old-fashioned way of shaving and create, in his words, "an idyllic male sanctuary," combining past civility with today's modern lifestyle.

Address 202B Elizabeth Street (near Spring Street), New York 10012, **Phone** +1 212.334.9495, www.nyshavingcompany.com, info@nyshavingcompany.com | **Transit** Subway: Bowery (J); Spring St (6), Bus: M 21, M 103 | **Hours** Mon–Fri 11am–8pm, Sat 10am–8pm, Sun 11am–7pm

69 __ Obscura Antiques & Oddities

A bazaar of the bizarre

This macabre little shop of horrors aptly occupies a former funeral home in the East Village. Its bizarre and extraordinary array of artifacts is scavenged from flea markets, antique shows, auctions, attics, and private collections from all over the globe. The modest-sized store, with its creaky wooden floors, has a dark and twisted atmosphere – an other-worldly universe of useless but irresistibly intriguing artifacts, that are even tantalizingly morbid.

Among Obscura's diverse curios, which Ripley (Believe It Or Not!) might dub *queeriosities*, you may find: taxidermied two-headed beasts, a preserved buffalo scrotum, a tribal penis sheath gourd, human and animal skulls and skeletons, antiquated medical probes, jarred piranhas and lizards, Victorian wigs, rectal dilators, autopsy and amputation tools, a mummy-head snow globe, nail-clipping art, a lobotomy ice-pick, a creepy crawling doll, glass eyeballs, leather frog purses, marbles entombing preserved insects, antique marionettes, and chocolate crow skulls.

One customer described its allure. "This place has it all! I felt like a kid in a candy store, walking around and around absorbing everything in sight. My 5-year-old son wanted to stay there all day!"

Anyone familiar with the Discovery Channel's *Oddities* TV show has already visited this freaky emporium, for Obscura's hunt for rarities is the focus of the series. It's not a place for everyone. But if your curiosity outweighs your squeamishness, your fantasies and imagination will not be disappointed. The knowledgeable shopkeepers are delighted to share the gory details and backstories of the dark pleasures their collection promises.

While prices may be understandably high for certain bizarre, unique collectibles, there are also relatively affordable tidbits for the tourist trade. And you can walk out with an Obscura tote bag to let the world know how truly weird you are.

Address 207 Avenue A (near 13th Street), New York 10009, Phone +1 212.505.9251, www.obscuraantiques.com, info@obscuraantiques.com | Transit Subway: 1st Ave (L), Bus: M8, M9, M14, M15, M101, M102, M103 | Hours Mon–Sat 12–8pm, Sun 12–7pm

70__ Off Broadway Boutique

Where theatricality rules the day

Owner Lynn Dell's favorite two words are *glamour* and *beauty* – and both words aptly apply to her. The Countess of Beauty (as she is known to fans) is a gorgeously flamboyant octogenarian who started her business fifty years ago and has seen it grow into an Upper West Side institution. Lynn is the personification of her own retail creation. With movie-star make-up and manicured multi-ringed fingers, she's always elegantly coifed or dramatically hatted, and accessorized to the hilt. Madame Dell looks like she's just stepped onto the set of an MGM film, ready for her next scene. As the best model for her shop's fancy and fanciful array of eye-catching fashions, she likes to say she dresses for 'the theater of life.'

Over the years this style maven has crisscrossed the globe in search of specialty jewelry and one-of-a-kind garments that befit celebrities and royalty, much of it edgy and often bordering on outrageous. At the salon-like shop with show tunes playing in the background, it's fun to explore colorfully bedecked counters and displays with goods from Tibet, Morocco, India, South America, Europe. You'll see styles you won't find elsewhere – sophisticated organza and silk jackets, exotic harem pants, trumpet skirts, coquettish berets and wide-brim straw or flowery and feathered *chapeaus*. Bold jewelry that makes a statement, baubles and bangles that demand attention – gold and onyx earrings, crystal-embedded bracelets, corkscrew brooches – all selected to appeal to fearless fashionistas with serious flair. Off Broadway's vintage section is full of surprises, and their custom design department can alter or create fashions to suit any taste.

Lynn's insightful advice applies to young and old alike. "Your attitude is your altitude, and every age is a triumph. Be beautiful now." So if you get a kick out of making an entrance and you crave caviar before noon – welcome to Ooh-la-la Land!

Address 139 West 72nd Street (near Broadway), New York 10023, Phone +1 212.724.6713, www.boutiqueoffbroadway.com, offbroadwayboutique@gmail.com | Transit Subway: 72 St (1, 2, 3, B, C), Bus: M 5, M 7, M 11, M 57, M 72, M 104 | Hours Mon–Fri 10:30am–8pm, Sat 10:30am–7pm, Sun 1–7pm

71 Oliver Moore Bootmakers

No business like shoe business

Did you know that shoes were made exactly the same for left and right feet until the mid-1800s? In 1878, Englishman Oliver Moore, founder of the venerable bespoke (made-to-order) shoe company, took his knowledge and love of the craft to America. His family was among the first to design shoes separately for each foot – before that, a shoe was just a shoe!

Today, the current owners, 'shoeman' Paul Moorefield, and footwear artist and designer Joan Silverman, along with a staff of veteran craftsmen, carry on the tradition of creating some of the most beautiful, custom-designed, hand-wrought shoes anywhere. The store also sells ready-made women's and men's shoes from leading high-end brands, but it's the bespoke business that distinguishes this elite shop. Through the slow, exacting process their artisans produce ten to twenty pairs a week.

For every client they take at least seven different measurements of each foot to produce the 'last' – that's the carved wooden personalized foot-shaped form around which handmade shoes are constructed. The labor involved in each custom order requires more than two hundred separate operations to make just one pair of shoes, usually taking about eight weeks.

Luxury and style come at a price. Men's shoes start at $2,200, not including the $1,000 cost of the one-time last, the template for all future orders. Women's shoes begin at $1,200. Apart from a long list of the rich and famous, their clients are people with chronic foot problems, and those wanting copies made of their favorite *old* shoes – out of style and irreplaceable.

The shop's elegant ambience is in tune with the Upper East Side's tony character, with oriental carpets and old-world period furniture. All told, what is it you're getting? A flawless fit. Pure comfort. The finest leathers (even ostrich and shark). And the ability to create any style you wish. The bespoke shoe experience bespeaks itself.

Address 856 Lexington Avenue (near 65th Street), New York 10065, Phone
+1 212.288.1525, www.olivermoorebootmakers.com, info@olivermoorebootmakers.com |
Transit Subway: 63 St-Lexington Ave (F); 68 St-Hunter College (4, 5, 6); 59 St-Lexington
Ave (4, 5, 6, N, Q, R), Bus: M 1, M 2, M 3, M 4, M 66, M 72, M 101, M 102, M 103 | Hours
Mon–Fri 10am–7pm, Sat 10am–5pm

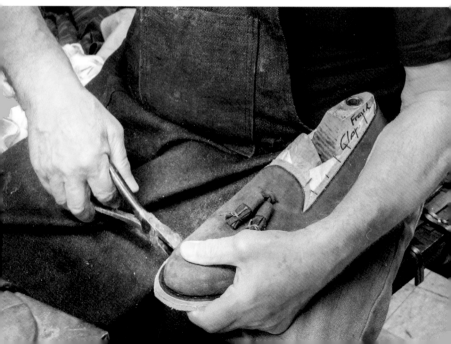

72 __ Orwasher's Bakery
Old-world breads in new New York

For generations the Orwasher family took great pride in using the same subterranean brick ovens and the same sourdough starter that their patriarch began with a century ago. Abraham Orwasher, newly arrived in America, started baking breads in the basement of the building where he lived in Yorkville – then a thriving Eastern European enclave.

Over time, with new generations making changes to the variety of breads, the ovens, and the management of the bakery itself, Orwashers has maintained its reputation for excellence among the many outstanding breads baked in New York. Adding to traditional rye and pumpernickel (and inventing raisin-pumpernickel in the 1940s), along came Irish soda bread, Italian *ciabatta*, wine and beer breads, and an array of whole-grain loaves. New ownership in 2007 introduced the artisan breads and prize-winning French baguettes. Once a week they honor the Orwasher legacy, started in 1916, by baking *challah* and other old-world loaves in the single remaining original oven in the basement.

The shop still serves the local community, though the bakery distributes their goods far and wide. But only at this store can you get one special treat: an individually made-to-order jelly donut – that fist-sized cakey bun infused with deliciousness. Every day a local pastry-maker supplies the donut puffs; an upstate farm kitchen delivers natural fruit preserves of just the right consistency to be squirt-gunned into fresh-baked, sugar-dusted buns. Pick your favorite flavor and watch as your porous puff is transformed into a mouthwatering treat.

Many consider Orwasher's the best jelly donuts anywhere. Made daily in small batches every morning, they're usually sold out by noon. What makes them so good? Maybe the pillowy texture, or the fruit-laden jelly, or the yummy squishiness created by a perfect ratio of jelly to donut. Each bite is more inviting than the last.

Mmmm… hungry yet?

Address 308 East 78th Street (near Second Avenue), New York 10075, Phone
+1 212.288.6569, www.orwashers.com, info@orwasherbakery.com | Transit Subway: 77 St
(6), Bus: M 15, M 31, M 72, M 79, M 101, M 102, M 103 | Hours Mon – Sat 7:30am – 8pm,
Sun 8am – 6pm

73 Pan American Phoenix Shop

South-of-the-border, right here in midtown

Just walking into this sunny outpost brightens your day, with cheerful primary colors and whimsical items everywhere you look. It's the city's oldest shop specializing in authentic Mexican clothing, textiles, jewelry, pottery, handicrafts, and folk art.

Inspired by her great love for Mexican style and tradition, Martha Bartos started the business in 1959, traveling to Mexico yearly in search of beautiful wares for her dream store. Daughter Mary joined her in 1976 and still runs the shop today, importing an extensive and eclectic assortment of Mexican and Latin-American treasures. She's proud of her reputation for high-quality goods – pure cotton clothing including embroidered dresses (many delightfully detailed with ribbon), peasant skirts, silky shawls, and buttoned Guayabera shirts. Colorful textiles displayed along the walls feature hand-loomed Oaxacan wool rugs, Guatemalan table linens, striped *serapes*, bolts of printed and woven cottons, and shiny patterned oilcloths sold by the yard.

Fine silver jewelry by top Mexican designers ranges from traditional to contemporary – earrings, bracelets, necklaces, pendants, and pins. For the *hombres* there are cufflinks, money belts, buckles, and key rings. Handpainted serving dishes and decorative pottery reflect hundreds of years of home and kitchen tradition. Luminous hand-blown and etched glassware, famous for its natural beauty (each piece taking six stages to produce!) comes in sizes from tumbler to goblet. Choose a single design or a fun mix-and-match assortment. Their decorative baskets, mirrors, lanterns, trays, or wall pieces can add elegant accents to your home. Mexican folk art in clay, wood, paper, and tin celebrates angels, nativities, and many traditional holidays and rituals.

One satisfied customer commented, "I have traveled to Mexico many times and never found a store there that collected as many great items all in one place!"

Address 857 Lexington Avenue (near 65th Street), New York 10065, Phone
+1 212.570.0300, www.panamphoenix.com, shop@panamphoenix.com | Transit Subway:
63 St-Lexington Ave (F); 68 St-Hunter College (4, 5, 6); 59 St-Lexington Ave (4, 5, N,
Q, R), Bus: M 1, M 2, M 3, M 4, M 66, M 72, M 101, M 102, M 103 | **Hours** Mon–Fri
10:30am–6:30pm, Sat 11am–6pm

74 Paragon Sports

Nonstop action

Walk through the entrance of this vast sports emporium and you immediately feel the energy. Flitting about in the maze of departments are runners, swimmers, hikers, goalies, ballplayers, snowboarders, and skaters. Contenders or champions, novices and pros, all converge here in search of the right equipment and apparel for their specialty. For sheer selection in virtually every sport, there is no other store like it in the city. This is the mecca of outdoor and athletic gear.

Paragon's four sprawling floors are stocked with state-of-the-art sporting goods, and attire from classic to cool. From marathoners to mountain climbers, cyclists to snorkelers, you'll meet athletes in every department. Paragon has the most innovative and technologically advanced products for a multitude of sports – footwear alone for more than twenty – priced from high-end to affordable. Globetrotting sports enthusiasts pursue their passion year-round. Experts in every field can assist with getting you outfitted correctly. Whether you're hiking the Himalayas, doing a triathlon, snowboarding in Aspen, or heading to Antarctica, they can suit you up. Wandering far afield or close to home, find the right tent for your trek or the best mat for yoga class.

For hands-on help – wether you're choosing a squash racquet or your kid's first League Little glove – experienced folks who really know your sport provide guidance and sensible advice. Here you can arrange for a NYC Parks Department tennis permit, join Paragon's Running Club, or sign up for ski/snowboard trips.

Combining abundant selection with expertise, this formula has worked for more than a hundred years – since 1908 when Paragon was founded by the family that still owns and runs it. The hustle and bustle, sales help on hand when you need it, jam-packed displays at every turn, and efficiently rapid check-out – all make Paragon a quintessentially New York experience.

Address 867 Broadway (at 18th Street), New York 10003, Phone +1 212.255.8889, www.paragonsports.com, customerservice@paragonsports.com | Transit Subway: 14 St-Union Sq (L, N, Q, R, 4, 5, 6); 14 St (E, F, M), Bus: M1, M3, M5, M7, M14, M23, M102, M103 | Hours Mon–Fri 10am–8:30pm, Sat 10am–8pm, Sun 11am–7pm

75__Patricia Field

The darling of daring

Fashion visionary Patricia Field began her career in 1966 in her Greenwich Village boutique, where she lived above the store, just a block away from Jimi Hendrix Electric Ladyland studios. Sixties psychedelic defined the style, and the Village was the hip scene. Now more in Lady Gaga mode nearly fifty years later, this downtown institution has remained a favorite of savvy celebs and flashy fashionistas. It's been a defining factor in the urban style of New York's glam-glitz nightlife, with everything from quirky to kinky to outlandish. Indelibly making her mark on pop culture, Field costumed TV's *Sex and the City*, earning her five Emmy nominations and one win.

Relocated in ultra-hip Noho, the multilevel store is as dazzling and freaky as ever. Some of Field's eccentric art collection lines the walls. Your senses are bombarded, like wandering through an acid dream with a trippy array of sexy clubwear, racy lingerie, unique legwear, edgy jewelry, and endless accessories. The shoes are from another planet – in unimaginable shapes, colors, and patterns. With all its funkiness, this is what happens when a fashion junkie collides with a drag queen's closet!

Prices go from cheap to outrageous, but each piece is chosen for its *hey-look-at-me* attitude and boldness. It's worth a trip just to check out the floor crew, whose get-up is wildly flamboyant and creative. These way-cool kids may look intimidating but – sometimes dancing spontaneously to the store's pulsing music with their platform shoes slapping the floor – they're fun and really helpful. Downstairs at the in-house hair salon you'll find experimental stylists with a flair for dare, plus a wig bar with its own specialist.

With any luck, you'll catch Patricia in the shop concocting bizarrely imaginative displays, meeting and greeting customers, and daring you to go ahead and try that dress on – "It's YOU, baby!"

Address 306 Bowery (near Houston Street), New York 10012, Phone +1 212.966.4066, www.patriciafield.com, customerservice@patriciafield.com | Transit Subway: 2nd Ave (F); Bleecker St (6); Broadway-Lafayette (B, D, M), Bus: M 5, M 15, M 21, M 103 | Hours Sun–Thurs 11am–8pm, Fri–Sat 11am–9pm

76__Peanut Butter & Co.

The incredible spreadable

Fact: peanut butter is neither butter nor nut (the peanut is actually a legume). Who knew?! It's actually a paste made of mashed-up roasted peanuts, first known to ancient Incas, that's been around in some form for nearly 3,000 years. Fast forward to its re-invention in late nineteenth-century America, and soon to become "as American as apple pie." For years, big brand companies mass-marketed the stick-to-the-roof-of-your-mouth spread we know today – traditionally smeared with jelly on white bread, aka the PB&J – but sometimes mixed with quirkier ingredients like mayonnaise, olives, onions, horseradish, or jalapeños.

Then in 1998 along came Lee Zalben, founder of Peanut Butter & Co., who was always the hands-down winner of his college dorm contests for the most inventive peanut butter sandwich. His childhood passion for the stuff led him to open an unpretentious, cozy sandwich shop in Greenwich Village that grew steadily more famous and successful. His secret? Yummy sandwich combos with catchy names like The Elvis (PB grilled with bananas, honey, and bacon), and Pregnant Lady (PB and pickles). And gluten-free, all-natural, newfangled flavors like delicious Dark Chocolate Dreams, spicy The Heat Is On, or honey-laced The Bee's Knees. At the shop you can enjoy Jerry Seinfeld's namesake concoction (on a bagel) or crunch on a PB&J Pretzel Sundae for dessert.

It wasn't long before devotees begged to take home his specialty peanut butters in quantity. So, by popular demand, the "Peanut Guy" as he became known, began jarring his nutty creations. Today, Peanut Butter & Co. sells ten mouth-watering flavors worldwide to over 10,000 stores. The owner is proud to say he uses only USA-grown peanuts in his products.

The sandwich shop has turned into a pilgrimage site for peanut butter lovers the world over. And with his exports, Lee's fulfilling his dream to spread peanut butter all over the globe.

Address 240 Sullivan Street (near West 3rd Street), New York 10012, Phone +1 212.677.3995, www.ilovepeanutbutter.com, customer.service@ilovepeanutbutter.com | Transit Subway: West 4 St (A, B, C, D, E, F, M); Christopher St-Sheridan Sq (1), Bus: M 1, M 2, M 3, M 5, M 8, M 20, M 21 | Hours Sun –Thurs 11am –9pm, Fri –Sat 11am –10pm

77 Pearl River

Not just a store, but a cultural bridge

When you step inside the storefront on Broadway, your mouth drops with the sheer size and scale of the space. Your eyes dance at the sight of so many thousands of items begging to be picked up, examined, experienced. Then you learn that above and below your head are two more full floors of Asian goods, from tiny decorative stones to colossal ceramic urns. What a culture shock!

Started in 1971, before the US and China had an established trade relationship, Pearl River was a pioneer when it opened its first retail store in New York. The founders, a small group of young Chinese men and women, believed that authentic goods from all over Asia would be the most natural and "humble" way to promote not only good business, but genuine intercultural understanding. The store was an instant success. And thus an early economic bridge was built between East and West.

Now, four decades later, Pearl River is New York's most celebrated Chinese department store. It offers a staggering assortment of traditional products – from the simple and practical to the chic, stylish, curious, and exotic. From trinkets to treasures, more than 15,000 separate items are priced from 50 cents to $5,000.

This 30,000-square-foot retail emporium invites urban trekkers from all over the world into the soul of the Far East, making it more than a store – rather a cultural banquet. With its large staff of Chinese-born Asians and hip second-generation Americans, Pearl River is at the vanguard of city chic. Since moving to its Soho location in 2003, the massive space has been wowing global tourists with its atmosphere, its modular décor, and sleek silvery interior waterfall.

Pearl River has been featured on various TV shows, among them Martha Stewart, Ming Tsai (cooking), and Oprah. No journey to the Big Apple is complete without a stop at Pearl River – a store that crosses oceans to bridge a cultural gap.

Address 477 Broadway (near Broome Street), New York 10013, Phone +1 212.431.4770, www.pearlriver.com, pearlriver@pearlriver.com | **Transit** Subway: Canal St (N, Q, R, A, C, E); Spring St (6); Broadway-Lafayette (B, D, F, M), Bus: M 5, M 20, M 21, M 103 | **Hours** Daily 10am–7:20pm

78__ The Pickle Guys

Barrels of fun

A visit to the Lower East Side would not be complete without a stop-and-taste at the Pickle Guys, where the breeze blows briny pickle smells up and down Essex Street. Owner Alan Kaufman, often elbow-deep in barrels of crunchy delight, takes pride in preserving not only cukes, but the tradition itself of kosher pickling. Now Pickle Guys is the only one still standing on a street once populated with picklers. Kaufman aims to keep his brimming barrels in their historic home.

But it's not just pickles anymore. Besides the usual sours and half sours, patrons can choose from a varied selection of cured vegetables and yes, even fruits – tomatoes in several varieties, green and black olives, mushrooms, celery, hot peppers, sweet kraut and sauerkraut, turnips, watermelon, mangoes, pineapples, and more, as Kaufman likes to get creative with his craft.

And what's the secret of the perfect pickle? An old Eastern European recipe. "Just the way mom used to make 'em," he reminisces. Carefully selected cucumbers sit in a salt brine with garlic and assorted spices, then are stored in large barrels to cure for anywhere from a day to three months, depending on the desired degree of sourness.

Kaufman is a purist. He uses the same pickling practices handed down for generations – without chemicals or preservatives – and operates under the strict supervision of a rabbi. The result yields a remarkably fresh product, with that perfect snap and spray in every bite. The fully soured pickles, in particular, make your mouth pucker with delight. It's a wonder that the amiable owner, after all these years in the brine, doesn't have a sour bone in his body! "I get a big kick when people take a bite and say, *Wow, this is good!*" grins the owner. "We kibitz with our customers and keep a happy atmosphere going. It's not really like work at all. It's a pickle party."

Address 49 Essex Street (near Grand Street), New York 10002, Phone +1 212.656.9739, www.pickleguys.com, sales@pickleguys.com | Transit Subway: Delancey St (F); Essex St (J, M, Z); Grand St (B, D), Bus: M9, M14A, M15, M22, B39 | Hours Sun–Thurs 9am–6pm, Fri 9am–4pm

79__PIQ

Take your pick, from cheap to chic

Feeling fanciful? Surprise someone you love – pick up a rubber-chicken handbag for your playful grannie, a mustache pacifier for your hip little toddler, a kinky artwork for an off-beat boyfriend. PIQ (as in 'PIQ a cool gift') is a quirky outpost where you'll discover unexpected items priced from a few dollars to several thousand. With over forty years of gift-industry experience, the owners aim to satisfy the whimsy of both young children and adult kids. There's something for everyone – from shop-savvy suburbanites, intense urban hipsters, to the most discriminating toy connoisseurs.

This shiny oasis in busy Grand Central Terminal offers a wildly colorful array of entertaining *tchotchkes*, designer toys, home accessories, pop-art originals, and esthetic artifacts acquired from all over the world. A fantastical zoo of African animals crafted in Kenya out of recycled rubber flip-flops will definitely tickle your funnybone. You can choose from affordable favorites like fish coin-purses and salami-note stickies; or from pricey artworks of limited-edition prints and sculptures by edgy local artists. As much a cutting-edge art gallery as an innovative gift shop, PIQ regularly schedules Meet the Artist events, inviting the public to hobnob with the creators of the imaginative pieces sold in the store.

The shop's eclectic choices are inspired by the street as well as by the museum, mixing the mundane with the unusual. Everyday wares are displayed side-by-side with designer goods, contemporary alongside vintage. Visitors, shoppers, and curious passersby duck in from the swirling mass of daily commuters to browse and find treats here for everyone, including themselves.

One thing is sure – stopping in here during your hectic day will bring a smile to your face. PIQ's selection appeals to the inner child in all of us, with fun, funny, and inventive goodies. It just can't fail to pique your curiosity!

80__Play @ Museum of Sex

X-rated, with impeccable taste

This playground for the senses is probably too kinky or kooky for a first date, but for close friends enjoying a *tête à tête* over a light lunch or a few drinks it's classy and casual and, well… different.

The ground floor of MoSex (Museum of Sex's cheeky nickname) is actually a triplex of intriguing shops: Nice & Sweet cafe, PLAY (a cozy wifi lounge by day, sultry cocktail den and bar by night), and the boutique, MoSexStore. If you're curious but self-conscious, enter at the cafe's discreet side street entrance and make your way into the other venues.

The idea was first conceived as an exhibit to offer visitors "an experience without boundaries, where imagination could run free and they could lick, sniff, bite, suck, and poke the art." This led to transforming the space into a garden of delights to titillate and tempt the senses with tantalizing tastes, textures, and aromas. The cafe serves snacks, lunch, wines, coffees. At the bar, evening drink and snack menus are designed to explore the relationship between food and sex, like the slurpy, slippery raw bar selections. If you're feeling lascivious, try the Lickable Skin cocktail (designed by artist Bart Hess, creator of Lady Gaga's *Born This Way* black-slime costume); it's served as a creamy white puddle on a skin-textured plate, and is meant to be lapped up.

The Den, a soft-lit version of erotically-charged college library stacks, is intimate yet academic. The books are all plain-brown-paper-wrapped; many are doodled or artist-altered with 3-D origami innards. Vintage girly magazines lay about on tables. Tiny brick-size peep-show videos wink from the walls. It's surreal, subtle, and sensual.

The museum shop has designer versions of sex toys, novelties, books, gifts, and souvenirs as well as outrageous wearable artpieces and fetish gadgetry, which can entertain you and your companion as a prelude to an intimate adventure – or just for fun.

Address 1 East 27th Street (at Fifth Avenue), New York 10016, Phone +1 212.447.PLAY, www.willyouplaywith.us, info@museumofsex.com | Transit Subway: 28 St (N, R, 1, 6), Bus: M 1, M 2, M 3, M 5, M 6, M 7, M 23, M 102, M 103 | Hours Cafe: Mon–Fri 7am–9pm, Sat–Sun 8am–9pm; Bar: Mon–Sat 5pm–2am, Sun 5pm–12am

81 The Porcelain Room

Serving up a traditional dish

A single gold-rimmed teacup – inscribed, monogrammed, and gifted to a family patriarch – inspired The Porcelain Room's founder Michael Koh, revealing to him the fascinating world of fine porcelain and kindling a lifelong passion. Out of curiosity he researched the heirloom's origin. As the intriguing history of European china unfolded, it ignited a desire to protect and share this specialized art form with the world. A vital aspect of his business is imparting an appreciation of this to his customers.

In this cozy shop with strains of classical music playing in the background, you feel the love. Its name is inspired by the various Porcelain Rooms in European grand palaces and estates of centuries past, when royalty and aristocracy valued Chinese and Japanese fine porcelain over the pottery and pewter then in use in Europe. These special rooms were dedicated to the display of elegant dinner services, precious vases, clocks, and figurines that reflected the particular style of the palace's interior decor, from baroque and rococo up to art deco. When Europe's royal houses began producing porcelain in the early 1700s, they primarily outfitted and stocked their own palaces. Porcelain Rooms soon held a rich variety of European-made porcelain, as well as oriental pieces and sets.

That elegant ambience is re-created in this charming, below-stairs shop, which displays not only beautiful, unusual antiques and collectibles from Europe and Asia, but also contemporary hand-crafted and painted porcelain from the world's best manufacturers. The shop's expert, engaging owners delight in assisting clients in the right choice of a new dinner or tea service. Individual pieces or full sets can be also customized for color, text, or monogram design. And wedding registries are welcome.

Even if you're not a collector, you'll feel what it's like to be treated like royalty when you visit The Porcelain Room.

Address 13 Christopher Street (near Greenwich Avenue), New York 10014, Phone +1 212.367.8206, www.theporcelainroom.com, info@theporcelainroom.com | Transit Subway: Christopher St-Sheridan Sq (1); West 4 St (A, B, C, D, E, F, M); 14 St (2, 3), Bus: M1, M2, M3, M5, M7, M8, M14, M20 | Hours Mon–Thurs 12–8pm, Fri–Sat 12–9pm, Sun 12–7pm

82 Porto Rico Importing Co.

Grinding out pure java joy

The intoxicating aroma of brewing coffee wafting out to the sidewalk is an inviting welcome mat for any coffee-lover. Once inside, the rich, warm atmosphere transports you to another era. This is what a traditional purveyor of coffees and teas should be. Rows of stenciled burlap bags bulging with roasted beans stretch the length of the store. Wooden shelves along the walls are stocked with a wide selection of loose teas, with exotic names like Hairy Crab Oolong, Pinhead Gunpowder, and Margaret's Hope Darjeeling.

In 1907, when Porto Rico Importing opened on Bleecker Street in what was then a thoroughly Italian neighborhood, it was just one of perhaps a dozen stores like it selling whole-bean coffee to the locals. Today it's the last one standing. Through generations of bohemians, beatniks, hippies, and now the dotcom crowd, Porto Rico has supplied beans to individual customers, cafes, and restaurants and been an integral part of the famous Greenwich Village coffee house scene.

There's a dizzying variety of beans and blends from every coffee-producing region in the world. Here you'll find every style of coffeemaker, espresso machine, brewing contraption, mug, and teapot, not to mention a tempting panoply of sweet treats – like coffee toffee and chocolate-covered espresso beans. They also carry a line of traditional Italian specialties: spices, dried mushrooms, syrups, digestive aids, and medicinal elixirs. It's a throwback to the old neighborhood, still with an Italian-American flavor.

Customer service is the crux of their success, according to Peter Longo, the third-generation owner. He trains his staff to be educated about their products and mindful of the patron's needs. They'll gladly give you a tour of the roasts if you're overwhelmed and can't decide what you're looking for in a customized brew.

Sample the coffee of the day and if you bring your own mug, say "refill" and it's only 65 cents! Can't beat that in a city where most coffee joints charge $2.50 and up for a cup of pure java joy.

Address 201 Bleecker Street (near Sixth Avenue), New York 10012, Phone
+1 212.477.5421, www.portorico.com, questions@portorico.com | Transit Subway:
West 4 St (A, B, C, D, E, F, M); Houston St (1), Bus: M 5, M 20, M 21 | Hours Mon–Sat
9am–9pm, Sun 12–7pm

83___Rudy's Hobby Shop

Everything old is new again

Astoria, Queens, is one of the city's trendiest new 'old neighborhoods.' Once an industrial working-class area (home to, among others, the Steinway piano factory), it now hosts Kaufman-Astoria, a movie/tv studio rivaling Hollywood, and the cool Museum of the Moving Image. Its bustling shopping streets are lined with a fascinating mixture of fading mom-and-pop shops, chic boutiques, wifi cafes, ethnic restaurants, and hip wine bars. Amidst this cacophony of then and now sits Rudy's, whose card reads *Hobby & Art & Religious Items*.

Incongruous? No. Rudy's Hobby Shop is glued together by the past. He has model kits of planes, trains, and automobiles; fine art supplies; milk crates brimming with used books and records; a religious statuary with relics and rosaries; and what Rudy calls 'floor toys' – miniature cars and soldiers for that rare kid who still seeks low-tech thrills. And it all works.

Its greatest allure is the atmosphere, like a big old attic full of mysterious treasures. Shelves and cases are crammed with cellophane-wrapped childhood memories, like paint-by-number sets. Vintage airplanes hang from the ceiling in suspended animation. Presiding over the eclectic curios is Rudy Cochran, a gentle, unassuming man whose business has evolved from serving ice cream fifty years ago to selling model trains to becoming a full-service hobby store. When a neighboring art supply house closed he bought up its inventory. Ditto for a religious articles store. Gradually Rudy's became a repository for, well… this 'n' that. That's his niche.

Devoted hobbyists are drawn to it, finding classic and current kits and materials hard to get elsewhere. Locals have always loved it. Couples come in and the mister buys hobby stuff while the missus buys rosary beads. All dread the day when Rudy decides to retire. Nothing will bridge the time-gap in Astoria the way this one-of-a-kind store does.

Address 35–16 30th Avenue (near 36th Street), Astoria 11103, Phone +1 718.545.8280 |
Transit Subway: 30th Ave (N, Q), Bus: M60, Q18, Q19, Q101, Q102, Q104 |
Hours Wed–Sat 11am–6:30pm

84 — Russ & Daughters

Smoked fish like you wouldn't believe!

When the original owner, Joel Russ, emigrated from Poland in 1907, he sold dried mushrooms from a pushcart on the Lower East Side. By 1914 Russ had set up his first shop, an appetizing store offering the finest quality smoked and pickled fish. Originally, for the largely Jewish population of the Lower East Side at that time, *appetizing store* was a shop that sold any foods eaten with bagels – largely smoked fish and dairy products – while *delicatessen* referred to stores that sold cured and pickled meats.

The problem was that Russ' gruff manner drove customers away. But he had three attractive daughters, and his good business sense prompted him to use these pretty maidens to serve up the fish – smoked slices of heaven for which he was to become renowned. The tactic worked, and making what was a bold move in 1933, Russ renamed the store to include "& Daughters" – possibly the first time this was done in what was a man's world of commerce.

Today, behind the glass display cases at Russ & Daughters, there is a sumptuous assortment of smoked salmon (at least eleven varieties), shimmering-gold stacks of whitefish, a mouthwatering assortment of pickled herrings, caviars, gefilte fish, and trout. You'll find flavored cream cheeses and fish salads. Across the aisle is a gleaming assortment of delicate pastries, dried fruits, nuts, chocolates, and old-fashioned candies.

The staff behind the counter is chatty and well versed in the intricacies of curing and pickling, the nuances of perfect slicing techniques and serving suggestions. They are happy to share their knowledge and skills with the bustling crush of customers from all over the world.

Little did Joel Russ know that his store would one day be lauded by such diverse sources as the Smithsonian Institute, the National Register of Historical Places, *New York Times*, National Public Radio, and even Martha Stewart! You better believe it!

Address 179 East Houston Street (near Allen Street), New York 10002, Phone
+1 212.475.4880, www.russanddaughters.com, info@russanddaughters.com | Transit
Subway: 2nd Ave (F); Delancey St (J, M, Z); Bleecker St (6), Bus: M15, M21, M103 |
Hours Mon–Fri 8am–8pm, Sat 8am–7pm, Sun 8am–5:30pm

85 Sakaya

An elegant course in the culture of sake

Nestled on a quiet street in the East Village, Sakaya is the story of a dream come true. Owners Rick and Hiroko believe the time is right for New York to have its first – and to date, only – shop specializing in premium sake. Rick's passion for the drink began in 2000 when he experienced a special Japanese dinner in New York where the food was paired with a selection of several different types of sake. It was a revelation when he sipped and sniffed the variety and versatility of this beverage – often referred to erroneously as *rice wine*. It was served slightly chilled and was nothing like that hot, overly alcoholic 'jet fuel' he had imbibed at so many Japanese restaurants during the eighties and nineties. In fact, sake is not a wine at all, but rather a brew, much like beer. "However," he points out, "it drinks like a fine wine."

As a longtime wine enthusiast, Rick was surprised to find that sake, too, had an alluring abundance of aromas and flavors – all from the deceptively simple combination of rice, water, yeast, and *koji* (a fermenting agent). That seminal experience launched him into a headlong pursuit of sake-tasting wherever the brew was available – and led him to more intense research sessions with his wife Hiroko at home. Born and raised in Japan, where sake is an integral part of the culture, Hiroko's reverence for it grew more organically over the course of her life.

At Sakaya the focus is on educating their customers, familiarizing them with the pleasures of sake, and pairing it with a variety of foods, even cheeses and desserts. Rick and Hiroko offer a learning experience that not only creates an appreciation of sake, but also of the culture from which it originates.

The cheerful owners feel that they are just scratching the tip of the 'sake iceberg' as they like to call it. There is always more to explore and learn – and they believe the fun is in sharing that knowledge with their patrons.

Address 324 East 9th Street (near Second Avenue), New York 10003, Phone +1 212.505.7253, www.sakayanyc.com, rick@sakayanyc.com | Transit Subway: Astor Pl (6); 8 St-NYU (N, R), Bus: M8, M14A, M15, M101, M102, M103 | Hours Mon–Sat 12–8pm, Sun 12–7pm

86__ Schaller & Weber

The best of the wurst

By the time Ferdinand Schaller arrived in New York in 1927, he was already a gifted *charcutier*, having begun his career at the age of fourteen as apprentice to a butcher and sausage-maker in Stuttgart, working alongside German masters. A decade later in New York he met similarly dedicated butcher Tony Weber, and together they formed a partnership. In 1937 they opened Schaller & Weber in Yorkville on the Upper East Side – at that time a German enclave known as Germantown. They were one of many such businesses in the ethnic neighborhood, making their own goods right in the store. An immediate success, their authentic European-style sausages and deli meats were being enjoyed by aficionados throughout the city, and later across the country and around the world. Over the years, Schaller & Weber products have repeatedly won gold and silver medals at international exhibitions in Holland, Austria, and Germany – a special honor for an American *charcutier*.

Schaller firmly believed "if you start with the best ingredients, use traditional, time-honored recipes, and take pride in your work, you will get the finest product." The brand's consistent high quality attests to that. Their bratwurst and other authentic sausages are on a par with any from Germany. Famous smooth and meaty pates include old favorites like Gold Medal and Oldenberger, plus the more recent Liver Pate with Truffles. They make over twenty varieties of sausage, nine different liverwursts, seventeen cold cuts, four bacons (the "triple-threat double smoked bacon" is a winner!), eight smoked meats, and fifteen cervelats and salamis. The glistening-white tiled shop is brimming with imported European foods of all kinds.

A family-run business for three-quarters of a century, they still offer every child a sample of their award-winning German bologna. "After all," they like to say, "kids are the hardest ones to please."

Address 1654 Second Avenue (near 86th Street), New York 10028, Phone +1 212.879.3047, www.schallerweber.com, info@schallerweber.com | **Transit** Subway: 86 St (4, 5, 6), Bus: M 15, M 86, M 102, M 103 | **Hours** Mon–Fr 9am–6pm, Sat 8:30am–6pm

87 Serengeti Teas & Spices

Tastes for people of taste

This intriguing Harlem tea shop sells hundreds of African custom-blended teas and other tantalizing, exotic libations. Watch at the tasting bar as they prepare your customized beverage, then sip it slowly at a cafe table. Meanwhile, enjoy a taste of African culture. Polished dark wood furniture is set against pale walls, and shelves are lined with ornate tea kettles. Woven baskets alongside wild-animal wood carvings sit among decorative spice jars.

Serengeti Teas & Spices founder and 'blend guru,' Caranda Martin – a chef and chemist by training – conjures up a wide variety of unique flavors for your sipping pleasure. He takes you on a culinary journey that begins with the huge handcrafted tea collection, derived from numerous small harvesters in Africa and South Asia. Add to this: superb hot chocolates, specialty coffees, select spices from other foreign and exotic lands, and limited-edition beverages blended seasonally. Take home your favorites.

Caranda learned to cultivate productive relationships with tea growers in Africa during travels through the continent with his grandmother, an herbalist. She taught him the art of 'whipping' tea using dried, powdered leaves, infusing boiling water, then quick-stirring with a long wooden spoon. Not your typical cup of tea.

The shop revitalizes an African gastronomical culture combining unlikely beverage flavors, such as wild berries and heart of palm served with baobab. Reservations can be made for private tastings. Or walk in any day of the week to sample and savor daily specials. Products can be purchased custom-blended by the ounce or in beautiful pre-packaged tins designed in striking African colors and patterns.

Says Caranda, "My goal is to transition you from the concrete jungle of New York City into an environment that is different, unexpected, and African. We want to take you on a little journey in Harlem through the taste of Africa."

Address 2292 Frederick Douglass Boulevard (near 123rd Street), New York 10027, Phone +1 212.866.7100, www.serengetiteasandspices.com, serengetiteasandspices@hotmail.com | Transit Subway: 125 St (A, B, C, D), Bus: M 3, M 10, M 60, M 100 | Hours Mon–Wed 7:30am–7:30pm, Thurs–Fri 8am–8:30pm, Sat 8:30am–9pm, Sun 9am–7pm

88 Silvana

A multi-dimensional Harlem experience

In this age of multiplicity, it comes as no surprise that an establishment like Silvana not only exists, but flourishes. The owners, Sivan and Abdel Ouedrago, set out to create an environment that would appeal to the wide range of tastes and appetites that define the flourishing Harlem culture of today.

When you first walk through Silvana's baby blue doors, one of the welcoming staff will quickly introduce you to all its hidden treasures. On the street level, Silvana is a cafe/boutique carrying an ever-changing selection of local and global goods – handmade jewelry from Israel; colorful Ethiopian bags and hats; t-shirts by a Harlem designer; home decor from India; Moroccan rugs and pillow covers; and quirky wooden dolls from Burkina Faso. The cafe serves a full menu of Middle Eastern food (such as *falafel*, *shawarma*, and *shakshuka*), fresh-brewed organic coffee and tea, as well as wine and beer.

Sit at one of the vintage wooden tables fitted with ingenious swivel seats, and you'll be joined by an eclectic mix of families, students, freelancers, and local characters taking advantage of the free wifi and affordable refreshments in the cafe. In the evening, music drifts from below. Venturing downstairs, you'll discover a bar and lounge with a nightly lineup of several live bands and a deejay. The cabaret-style tables near the stage are decorated with images that evoke the sights, sounds, and smells of a Middle Eastern market. Towards the back of the lounge the Moroccan-style tray tables are surrounded by long benches and low stools – making it the perfect place to share a few dishes and drinks with new or old friends. Here you can enjoy the same fine food as upstairs, along with one of fourteen craft and traditional draft beers (try the Stone Arrogant Bastard and, if you dare, the Delirium Tremens). Juggling all the choices at Silvana, you can satisfy many desires at once.

Address 300 West 116th Street (near Frederick Douglass Blvd), New York 10026, Phone +1 646.692.4935, www.silvananyc.com, silvanabooking@gmail.com | Transit Subway: 116 St (A, C, D), Bus: M2, M3, M7, M10, M116 | Hours Cafe/Boutique: Daily 8am–10pm, Restaurant/Lounge: Sun–Thur 4pm–2am, Fri–Sat 4pm–4am

89__Sleep Studio

Yielding to the arms of Morpheus

"Sleep is not just a speed bump, where you slow down for an instant before resuming your full-throttle life. It means taking the time to wind down and prepare for sleep, both physically and mentally," advises Michael Rothbard, president of Sleep Studio.

There's a growing awareness of the importance of sleep to health and success, and the many benefits of happy slumber. How your environment prepares you – from furnishings and room lighting to sleepwear and surrounding sounds and scents – is vital to a good night's rest. The company uses sleep studies to learn more about it. And while technology and innovation contribute to the science of sleep, the end result should still be fun, sensual, and indulgent. But the store's mission is not to arouse – rather to relax. Because slumber is such an intimate experience, they reach out personally to clients to understand their lifestyle patterns, offering various approaches that remove barriers to deep, restorative sleep.

This specialty sleep company's flagship store in Soho is in a chic, high-ceilinged, wide-open space, designed in neutral shades and natural textures (like lofty feather-covered pendant lights). Sip a cup of herbal brew as you browse the collection of quality bedroom furnishings, bedding accessories, luxury sleepwear and loungewear for men and women, soothing teas, and a select apothecary of calming scents, and bath and beauty products.

The company's motto is *Sleep Beautifully*. They want to shamelessly pamper you into somnolence – with posh cashmere slippers, silk chemises, mohair throws, and Siberian goose down pillows. They feature a premium German-engineered bed with adjustable under-the-mattress discs that fine-tune comfort to your body. It's a sleep system designed to "fit you as personally as a custom garment."

In a store that specializes in everything luxurious and cuddly for the bedroom, going to bed becomes simply irresistible.

Address 73 Wooster Street (near Spring Street), New York 10012, **Phone** +1 212.756.1280, www.sleepstudio.com, soho@sleepstudio.com | **Transit Subway:** Spring St (C, E); Canal St (A, 1); Prince St (N, R), **Bus:** M 5, M 20, M 21 | **Hours** Mon−Sat 11am−7pm, Sun 12−6pm

90 Sockerbit Swedish Candy

A treat for the eyes and yummy for the tummy

Entering this nearly empty shop might remind you of Hollywood's ethereal depictions of heaven – bright white, soft light, pristine, alluring. Monochromatic except for the main attraction: the riot of color in the candy bins, all 168 of them. Along one cornucopian wall is a spectrum of glittering goodies in a rainbow of pastels and primary colors. Each bin is loaded with bite-size Scandinavian treats, called *smågodis*, and they represent the collective sweet tooth of Swedish, Danish, Norwegian, and Finnish candy traditions. They come in all shapes, sizes, and textures – gummy, sticky, gooey, chewy, mushy, creamy, crunchy, jelly – and in all imaginable flavors.

Many are candies you've never tried before and have names that tickle the American tongue – *hallonbåytar* (raspberry boats), *stora surskallar* (big sour skulls) and *bumlingar jordgubb* (strawberry boulders). Some you can't find elsewhere: chocolate-covered muesli, salty octopus-shaped licorice, caramel fudge with raisins, saffron suckers, chocolate-covered liquid mints, and liquor-flavored treats.

The idea is to make every candy-lover's dream come true – the chance to fill a personal goody bag with a mix of dozens upon dozens of taste treats. (On Saturdays in Sweden, children are allowed to do just that, and it's the highlight of the week!) Happily, and healthily, Sockerbit sweets contain high-quality ingredients, natural coloring, and no trans fats. And sweet is not the only flavor – you can choose from sour, salty, fruity, licorice, chocolaty, and the list goes on.

Sockerbit translates to "sugar cube," the inspiration for the store's design (as well as the name of one of its popular candies, a white-cubed marshmallow). It's an experience just to be inside the shop, gleaming and stark and tasteful and welcoming – and oh so Scandinavian! At Sockerbit, environment and product are uniquely combined to make it a colorful smorgasbord of heavenly treats.

Address 89 Christopher Street (near Seventh Avenue), New York 10014, **Phone** +1 212.206.8170, www.sockerbit.com, hello@sockerbit.com | **Transit** Subway: Christopher St-Sheridan Sq (1); West 4 St (A, C, E, B, D, F, M), Bus: M 5, M 8, M 20 | **Hours** Sun–Thurs 11am–8pm, Fri–Sat 11am–9pm

91__Stick, Stone & Bone

Giving off good vibrations

When Stick, Stone & Bone first opened in 1990, New-Age healing was a novelty, without the credibility it enjoys today. Still, enough followers of alternative practices have kept it alive so that now it's a respected resource for professional healers, shamans, Reiki practitioners, and other proponents of wellness therapies.

The superstars here are the crystals, fastidiously labeled with their properties and uses. But you don't need to understand *why* a rock makes you feel good. "The stones read your needs. It's like having a conversation with elements of the earth," believes Linda Curti, one of the owners. She and Yolanda Miller turned their fascination with the healing properties of natural elements into a one-stop shop for useful tools on your mystical journey through life.

Incense uplifts the spirit as you enter the twinkly-bright store whose surroundings resonate with positive energy. It might be the crystals, or the wall of webbed dream-catchers – but it's also the vibes from the folks who work there. The staff is not just enthusiastic, they're truly knowledgeable and can guide you to the appropriate choices. A customer about to buy tarot cards was asked, "These cards are for you, right?" The answer was yes. "That's good, because you should never give them as gifts. Tarot readers must pick out their own decks."

Choose from ritual incense, scented candles, handmade jewelry, Native-American feathers, raw and polished stones, icons, rare gems and minerals, medicine bags, boxes of herbs, and smudging fans. While most items at Stick, Stone & Bone are used for psychic awareness, wellness therapies, and meditation, many also appeal to curious collectors and creative gift shoppers. Even if the intended recipient isn't into spiritualism, everyone is attracted to the warmth of an aromatic candle or a lovely piece of jewelry – that just happens to vibrate with magical effects!

Address 111 Christopher Street (near Hudson Street), New York 10014, Phone
+1 212.807.7024 | Transit Subway: Christopher St-Sheridan Sq (1); West 4 St
(A, B, C, D, E, F, M), Bus: M5, M8, M11, M14, M20 | Hours Sun–Fri 12–8pm,
Sat 12–9pm

92 _ Story

Where change is the only constant

Businesses come and go in New York in the blink of an eye. One week the corner store is a cupcake shop, the next week it's for rent, a month later it's a nail salon. Such is the fickle retail trade. What's the secret to success? Maybe the trick is to keep it fresh... but how? Keep them guessing. Reinvent yourself.

So Story does exactly that every six to eight weeks. It's perfectly situated to attract an ever-changing stream of customers for its ever-changing identity. It is located near Chelsea art galleries, the hip Meatpacking District, and right opposite the High Line, New York's most trafficked new tourist destination.

"Retail is stale," says Rachel Schechtman, owner of Story, which was profitable in its first year. "My rule is to have a strong surprise and delight factor." Her years in corporate branding made her re-think brick-and-mortar store models. *Forbes* was impressed: "The new concept store has turned New York City retail on its head."

Think of merchandising like a magazine publisher, focusing on a different theme in every issue. Or an art gallery owner mounting a new show. Come up with a compelling story line, redesign the sales environment, restock with compatibly-themed merchandise, hold exciting related in-store events – and *voilà!* A new store at the old address every few months!

Past Story themes include Love, Color, NYC, and Made in America. To pay for transitions, Story finds corporate sponsors who want to reach customers attracted to the new venues. Benjamin Moore Paints came on board for Color Story, recast the store's decor, and hosted a talk on wall color and mood changes. Nerve.com, an online magazine and dating site, sponsored Love Story, offering free subscriptions to patrons. Community-minded with a conscience, Story seeks out small brands and start-ups to bring fresh ideas and products onto the marketplace.

Just don't ask what the next concept will be – it's a surprise!

Address 144 Tenth Avenue (at 19th Street), New York 10011, Phone +1 212.242.4853,
www.thisisstory.com, hello@thisisstory.com | Transit Subway: 14 St (A, C, E, L), Bus:
M 11, M 14, M 20, M 23 | Hours Call for current hours

93__Strand Bookstore

A booklover's treasure house

Named after the famous publishing street in London, the Strand Bookstore was born in 1927. It was just one among 48 downtown book vendors on Book Row, which started in the 1890s and gradually dwindled over the years. The original owner, Ben Bass, pursued his vision to have a store where used books would be cherished and booklovers could congregate. The Strand quickly became a Greenwich Village institution for writers as well as readers to meet, sell their books, and hunt for hidden treasures.

Today the Strand has 2.5 million used, new, and rare volumes – "over 18 miles of books," they proudly boast. Outside, on 12th Street, there's always a cluster of booklovers combing through the dollar carts for bargains and the occasional overlooked gem. Hidden in plain sight on the lower level, look for this secret stash: several aisles of reviewers' copies of recent books (some bestsellers!) marked down to half-price.

But one of the greatest features of the Strand is its third-floor Rare Book Room. Walking into this archival space is like stepping into the literary salon of a past era. Bathed in natural daylight, leather-bound classics line the walls from top to bottom. The original 1901 floorboards add vintage charm to this airy loft. The historic room is home to a collection of one-of-a-kind publishing rarities, from printing proofs and first editions to author-signed books and manuscripts – such as a Christie's dress-collection catalog autographed by Princess Diana; or books signed by Einstein, Mark Twain, or James Joyce. The collection is constantly changing and growing. The venerated room is the site of weekly readings by literary luminaries to which the public is invited, and it hosts prestigious book-launch parties for new releases.

The Strand is proud of its reputation as a community bookstore serving Greenwich Village – but also as a citywide and world-renowned treasure chest for scholars and bibliophiles.

Address 828 Broadway (at 12th Street), New York 10003, Phone +1 212.473.1452, www.strandbooks.com, strand@strandbooks.com | Transit Subway: 14 St-Union Sq (4, 5, 6, N, Q, R, L), Bus: M1, M2, M3, M8, M14, M102, M103 | Hours Mon–Sat 9:30am–10:30pm, Sun 11am–10:30pm

94 Streit's Matzos

The taste of an ancient memory

Since 1925, Aron Streit's family has been proudly producing their kosher matzos for Jewish customers in New York – and now all across America and in select foreign lands. Currently run by the fourth generation (with the fifth waiting in the wings), Streit's Matzos still follows the original baking techniques and religious practices of their Old World heritage. This is the last family-owned matzo company in the U.S., others having sold out to large corporations. Hands-on Streit family members – granddaughters and great-grandsons of the founder – hope to pass their tradition down to future generations, encouraging them to maintain Jewish values and rituals.

Still utilizing some of the matzo-making machinery great-grandpa Aron installed early last century, Streit's mixes only flour and water to create the biblically correct recipe for *unleavened bread* (no yeast). Hurriedly fleeing from slavery in ancient Egypt, the Israelites had no time to let dough rise, which resulted in desert-baked flatbread, or matzo – eaten today as it was thousands of years ago.

Some modern varieties – like Mediterranean matzo with sun-dried tomatoes – have been added to traditional ones. All are kosher, blessed by rabbis on the premises. Factory and retail shop are at the original site on the Lower East Side, once the heart of New York's Jewish community. The shop also carries an array of other traditional foods like egg noodles, borscht, matzo-ball mix, potato pancake *(latke)* mix, gefilte fish, macaroons, and more. Their expanded product line includes Asian and Middle Eastern foods.

You can peer through the shop's large glass windows to watch as freshly baked matzos march off the conveyor belt into the hands of workers stacking them for packaging. If you're lucky and can catch the eye of one of these gents, perhaps he'll offer you a crisp, hot taste treat. Literally, you will never eat a fresher matzo!

Address 148–154 Rivington Street (near Suffolk Street), New York 10002, Phone +1 212.475.7000, www.streitsmatzos.com, info@streitsmatzos.com | Transit Subway: Delancey St (F); Essex St (J, M), Bus: M 9, M 14, M 15, M 21 | Hours Mon–Thurs 9am – 4:30pm

95 Surma Ukrainian Shop

Where an Easter egg can save the world

New York is home to one of America's largest Ukrainian communities. From the 1870s, this culture occupied an enclave in the East Village known as Little Ukraine. Most immigrants have left, but the centerpiece of that ethnic community, St. George Ukrainian Church, still draws them back at Christmas and Easter holidays.

Opposite the church is a little shop whose original 1918 sign reads Surma Book & Music Co. Founder Myron Surmach, grandfather of the current owner, supplied his countrymen with newspapers, books, and other items from 'home.' Now a gift shop, it's stocked with so many traditional crafts and relics that you'll feel like you've landed in Eastern Europe.

Browse a colorful collection of handcrafted wares: woven kilims, embroidered folk blouses, *matryoshka* nesting dolls, painted eggs, religious icons, musical instruments, carved boxes, and ceramic dishware. Until his passing at age 98, the elder Surmach was also a devoted beekeeper, so a specialty of the shop is a selection of pure honeys brought in from upstate New York. They sell books in English and Ukrainian on the country's history, culture, traditions, and holidays. You'll find popular and classical music of the region, videos, and greeting cards.

Surma's painted Easter eggs, or *pysanky*, hold a particular fascination. Mystical powers of creation are associated with the egg. According to folklore, the fate of the world depends on perpetuating the custom of elaborately decorating them. As long as this custom goes on, so does life on earth. Should the practice cease, Evil in the guise of a vicious monster will encompass and destroy the planet. With an abundance of *pysanky*, Love conquers Evil and the world is safe.

You'll find an array of intricately decorated goose, chicken, wooden, and miniature eggs. Or buy wax, dyes, and all other supplies to craft your own *pysanka* – and keep us all out of harm's way!

Address 11 East 7th Street (near Third Avenue), New York 10003, Phone +1 212.477.0729, www.surmastore.com, surma@brama.com | **Transit** Subway: Astor Pl (6); 8 St-NYU (N, R), Bus: M1, M3, M5, M8, M15, M102, M103 | **Hours** Mon–Fri 11am–6pm, Sat 11am–4pm

96_ Sutton Clock Shop
Time marches on

Entering this tiny shop is to revisit the pre-digital past, when clocks had a voice of their own. They ticked and gonged and made ratchety noises when they were wound. They fill the cozy space – clocks of all kinds, ranging from stately nineteenth-century grandfathers to wind-up bedside alarm clocks of the 1960s. It's rich with the sounds of time, as clocks tick out the seconds and chimes sound on every quarter hour.

Knud Christiansen had been a world-class oarsman competing on the Danish crew team in the 1936 Berlin Olympics, when Hitler was in power. During the war he joined the Danish underground, rowing Jews to safety across the Baltic Sea at night, eluding German ships. Afterwards, he emigrated to the United States, opening Sutton Clock Shop in 1967. Christiansen – whose skill for repairing clocks and barometers was honed in pre-WWII Denmark – began his business on Lexington Ave and 61st Street where his sign, a giant pocket watch outside his second-story window, was a visual landmark for nearly half a century. Knud died in 2012 at age 97, and the shop moved to its Yorkville location.

Two of his sons continue the tradition, Sebastian being one of a few horologists in New York. Since childhood he'd absorbed his father's old-world craft, using the same tools as his master, tools clockmakers created centuries ago.

Half of Sutton Clock's business is retail, the other half is repair. Many clocks in the store are valuable antiques. "Everything can be fixed," says Sebastian with pride. He loves his job because there's no template. One has to get into the mindset of each clockmaker, see what his little quirk was. "There's a peaceful Zen to it. You tinker your way to solving the problem."

Sutton Clock Shop is a place where as time passes, it paradoxically stands still. Many of the clocks are there because they are – or were – disused and broken. Sebastian's mission? Keep the hands of time moving.

Address 218 East 82nd Street (near Third Avenue), New York 10028, Phone +1 212.758.2260, www.suttonclocks.com, info@suttonclocks.com | Transit Subway: 86 St (4, 5, 6), Bus: M 15, M 79, M 86, M 98, M 101, M 102, M 103 | Hours Tue–Fri 11am–4pm

97 — Tannen's Magic

Now you see it, now you don't

In 1925, the year before Houdini's sudden death and perhaps the peak of magic's popularity in America, an entrepreneurial young amateur named Louis Tannen began selling magic tricks on the street. First in a humble Brooklyn storefront, he later moved his shop to Manhattan among many competitors. Now the oldest professional magic shop in New York City, it is one of the few remaining. It's still a gathering place for novice magicians and a magnet for pros who come to check out the latest innovations. In an environment where knowledge translates to power, they all come to ultimately out-trick their hocus-pocus peers.

Tannen himself was a flamboyant performer who dazzled American soldiers, entertaining the troops overseas during WWII. As an inveterate inventor of new tricks, he began manufacturing equipment and props – inexpensive pocket tricks at first, then elaborate stage-sized illusions.

The store's black interior is understated. On one side there's an interesting display of stage props – swords, mystery boxes, flame and flower illusions. On another are shelves of instructional books and DVDs. Along the back, endless rows of drawers hold myriad marvels – from trick card decks to vanishing doves. On a black demo table amateurs can test their skills on one another or on unsuspecting browsers. In a collector's corner there's a framed letter signed by Houdini himself. People flock here from all over for demonstrations and scheduled lectures by well-known magicians. And wannabe wizards should inquire about Tannen's Magic Camp, a world-famous summer program training youngsters to hone their craft, choosing either close-up or stage magic.

The skilled staff gladly demonstrates any trick that interests you. No high-pressure sales talk here. They want you to feel at home and have fun. When you finally do tear yourself away, you'll experience one last trick: Tannen's disappears behind you!

Address 45 West 34th Street, Suite 608 (near Sixth Avenue), New York 10001 Phone +1 212.929.4500, www.tannens.com, info@tannens.com | Transit Subway: 34 St-Herald Sq (N, Q, R, B, D, F, M); 34 St-Penn Sta (1, 2, 3), Bus: M 1, M 3, M 4, M 5, M 7, M 20, M 34 | Hours Mon–Fri 11am–6pm, Sat–Sun 10am–4pm

98__ Tender Buttons

Little things mean a lot

In an eloquent tribute, one appreciative patron wrote: "You are a testimony to the magic of details, small gestures, and our resounding humanity in a world too often full of bravado, loudness, and big overtures." In an age when bigger is often assumed to be better, it's important – and fun – to celebrate the small and seemingly insignificant.

Tender Buttons is more than a quaint button shop – it's a time capsule. This narrow little store with antique furnishings has an exhibit wall of framed button sets on different themes from various periods: Victorian *Alice in Wonderland* characters, regimental brass closures from uniforms of forgotten wars, eighteenth-century hand-painted pastorals. History comes alive with the relevance and implications of this indispensable little fastener that has for centuries literally held civilizations together.

Sorted by color, size, style, shape, material, and theme, thousands of them live here in tiny boxes, row upon row, covering an entire wall. Four hundred kinds of blazer buttons alone! Buttons of ivory, porcelain, glass, Bakelite, Wedgwood, plastic, wood, even precious metals and stones. Many exquisitely crafted and imaginatively designed, they reveal our inherent need to embellish the minutia of our lives, to find beauty in the commonplace.

Aptly, the shop borrowed its name from a 1914 Gertrude Stein series of poems ruminating on mundane objects. Founded in 1964, and still run by Millicent Saffro, a former antiques restorer, the setting is a modest townhouse on the Upper East Side. Tender Buttons is the go-to place for designers, costumers, tailors, knitters, and collectors. And history buffs get a unique perspective on everyday life.

You may be replacing a lost button, restyling a vintage garment, or giving a new personality to a favorite old coat – you'll find it here. Come in, loosen your jacket, and thread your way through the history of button culture.

Address 143 East 62nd Street (near Lexington Avenue), New York 10065, Phone
+1 212.758.7004, www.tenderbuttons-nyc.com, info@tenderbuttons-nyc.com | Transit
Subway: 63 St-Lexington (F); 59 St-Lexington (4, 5, 6, N, Q, R), Bus: M 1, M 2, M 3, M 4,
M 15, M 31, M 57, M 66, M 101, M 102, M 103 | Hours Mon – Fri 10:30am – 6pm,
Sat 10:30am – 5:30pm

99_ Textile Arts Center

Where creativity looms large

If you don't know your warp from your weft, this place can help. Get savvy about all things textile – from actually creating a fabric by weaving, felting, or machine-knitting to adorning it with block-printing, embroidery, or natural dyes. Work with silks, leathers, or braided fibers. Learn to make a thing of beauty out of – literally – rags. Or, if you're not particularly craftsy, come in to browse the lovely handmade wares in their chic boutique.

There's a rainbow array of textile-based goods: unique garments, totes and bags, jewelry, wall hangings, sculpture, handmade gifts – all created by TAC instructors, students, residents, and friends. If you're already a hands-on artisan you'll appreciate the selection of textile-related supplies like natural dyes, cone yarns for looms, embroidery materials, and instructional books.

Nestled in the heart of Greenwich Village, this little workspace and shop, reminiscent of an artist's atelier, is an offshoot of TAC's flagship Brooklyn location, which houses artist-in-residence studios, a flourishing natural dye garden, and offers adult classes in every fathomable textile technique. The brick-walled studio in the Village is an urban-sized version, offering shorter classes designed for the busy after-work set. After-school sessions for youngsters five and up teach kids how to sew clothing, dye with plants, make sculpture out of cloth, and experiment with other textile crafts.

The Textile Arts Center is a hub of activity for the sustainable design community. The flexible nature of its studio space makes it a perfect venue for clothing industry events after hours. For example, the public is occasionally invited to browse independent designers' trunk shows or attend lectures on the use of natural dyes in the manufacture of clothing.

Weave your way to this colorful little shop and you may even be inspired to test the fabric of your own creativity.

Address 26 West 8th Street (near MacDougal Street), New York 10011, Phone
+1 646.225.6554, www.textileartscenter.com, info@textileartscenter.com | Transit Subway:
West 4 St (A, B, C, D, E, F, M); Christopher St–Sheridan Sq (1); 8 St–NYU (N, R); Astor
Pl (6), Bus: M1, M2, M3, M5, M8 | Hours Mon–Fri 10am–9pm, Sat–Sun 10am–6pm

100 Tiny Doll House

Lilliputian living

The phrase "attention to detail" springs to mind as you meander around this little shop, mesmerized by the variety and exquisite quality of the miniatures displayed like tiny museum gems. Nearly every aspect of home life is replicated here, mostly in one-twelfth the size of the real thing. From backyard barbecues to brocaded boudoirs, kiddy parties to kitchen pantries, with all the teensy accessories needed to breathe life into a scale model – pigeons, pastries, golf clubs, lacy hankies. Even a miniature dollhouse within a dollhouse, for the toy children playing on its porch.

Snuggled into a quiet Upper East Side street, Tiny Doll House is the only independent shop of its kind left in the city, where once there were several. Most dollhouse businesses have switched to e-commerce, but owner Leslie Edelman feels there's nothing like the real thing, up close and personal. He loves how customers delight in handling the diminutive objects and admire elaborately decorated period tableaus – medieval to modern – displayed along an entire wall.

Edelman's former career in interior design led to a passion for the craft when he first built a dollhouse for his niece. Loving the process of making a fantasy micro-world for a little girl, he started collecting, crafting, and selling. And opened a store to share his treasures. Children (yes, of all ages), architects, craftspeople, hobbyists, model-makers, and passersby are all enthralled by the whimsy and perfection of these mini-replicas. Some are simple manufactured pieces, others are individually handcrafted by artists and artisans, sometimes taking months to create. They're priced from a few dollars to a few thousand, and come from around the globe.

Perhaps the attraction is about living vicariously in a perfect world of your own creation. You may live in a cramped studio apartment, but you can furnish your lavish toy palace any way you like.

Address 314 East 78th Street (near Second Avenue), New York 10028, Phone
+1 212.744.3719, www.tinydollhouseny.com, info@tinydollhouseny.com | Transit Subway:
77 St (6), Bus: M 15, M 31, M 72, M 79, M 101, M 102, M 103 | Hours Mon–Sat
11am–5pm

101_ Tisane Pharmacy & Cafe

Tea and empathy

From the outside, this shop is not unlike many small neighborhood pharmacies. But appearances can be misleading. Once inside, you realize you've found a unique respite. A sense of nostalgia is instantly aroused in those who visit – there's no denying the charm of little cafe tables that greet you at the door, or the half-dozen tall stools inviting you to sit at the colorful tea bar laden with healthy goodies. From the personable expert pharmacists and staff who cater to every customer, to the familiar voices of locals chatting over a morning beverage and pastry, this is truly a spot where you'll feel welcome and well attended.

The tea bar offers sixty different loose-leaf teas (many herbal remedies among them), a daily choice of brewed organic coffees, fresh fruit smoothies, heavenly pastries, and even the traditional New York chocolate egg cream. Tisane could equally pass for a new-age tea shop or a 1950s American pharmacy-luncheonette. You won't just find run-of-the-mill chain store brands here, but rather a selection of the best organic, homeopathic, and often hard-to-find imported products other druggists don't carry.

Founded by two European pharmacists in 2011, the inspiration for Tisane comes at a time when superstore pharmacies are on the rise and small independent ones are sadly becoming extinct. The owners saw a need to bring the drugstore back to what it used to be – but then added a soupçon of international flair. Their vision was to create a place emphasizing natural care, where customers would have a real relationship with their pharmacist, where people would find their favorite imported health products – and where locals would enjoy an authentic neighborhood spot, reading the *New York Times* over a freshly brewed tea or coffee.

There is a sense of enchantment at Tisane Pharmacy & Cafe. You'll inevitably find that it offers more of a treat than merely a treatment.

Address 340 East 86th Street (near First Avenue), New York 10028, Phone
+1 212.517.0037, www.tisanepharmacy.com, info@tisanepharmacy.com | Transit Subway:
86 St (4, 5, 6), Bus: M 15, M 31, M 86 | Hours Mon – Fri 7:30am – 8pm, Sat 8am – 7pm,
Sun 10am – 6pm

102 Les Toiles du Soleil

Let the sun shine in

Think sunny thoughts: beach umbrellas in the sand; striped awnings flapping in the breeze; summery espadrilles along the Cote d'Azur. Be instantly transported to the bright ambience of the South of France inside this uncommonly cheery Chelsea shop, whose name says it all: Fabrics of the Sun. Surrounded by stripes and more stripes, in color combinations to make you smile, browse the beautiful fabrics and dry goods that have been coming off the old-style looms of the same factory for 150 years.

Since the 1860s this company has produced canvas for the classic rope-soled summer footwear worn by men and women alike – espadrilles. Situated in the Catalan region of southwest France, their factory was the first to bring power looms to the area, and it still weaves the finest pure cotton canvas, durable enough for both indoor and outdoor use. You'll find it here in candy-flavor stripes, woven to a 72-inch width to fashion into upholstery, curtains, window or shower treatments, or virtually any other use that demands both durability and style. The shop also features Sunbrella weather-resistant cloth for furnishings that are destined for prolonged exposure to the elements – like their cushion cubes that make great side tables for the canvas-sling chair nestled beneath a shady patio umbrella. All in multicolor stripes, of course.

Besides the long rolls of fabrics lining the shop's walls, there's an assortment of rainbow-dipped gifts – iPad covers, totes, baby booties and sunhats, stripey stuffed bears, chef's aprons, and kitchen linens like table runners, cocktail napkins, and oven mitts. All accessories are handmade in the store and can be customized.

Today, new apartments have more outdoor space then ever, if only a tiny, precious balcony. In a city where black is famously the color of choice, this shop is the paintpot at the end of the rainbow. Dip your brush and light up your palette.

Address 261 West 19th Street (near Eighth Avenue), New York 10011, Phone
+1 212.229.4730, www.lestoilesdusoleilnyc.com, info@lestoilesdusoleilnyc.com |
Transit Subway: 18 St (1); 14 St (2, A, C, E); 8th Ave (L), Bus: M 7, M 11, M 14, M 20 |
Hours Mon – Sat 12 – 7:30pm, Sun 12 – 6pm

103__ Toy Tokyo

Enter – and you're a kid again

A crayon-color parade of giant pop-culture characters watches over the entrance to Toy Tokyo, and it's a perfect welcome to this fantasyland. You're instantly struck by a glittery kaleidoscope of toys and collectibles. Some people pause to take it all in at once, but it's impossible – the overwhelming volume of international toys washes over you like a tidal wave. Lost in the surf, you're tempted to spend an afternoon browsing in a sea of mini-figures and amusing characters from every genre of any generation.

Toy Tokyo opened in 2000, modeled after similar stores in Japan with bright lights, crammed arrangements, and overflowing toy bins. Since then it's earned a reputation for having the most unique inventory of collectibles in the city, featuring newly iconic as well as classic items from cartoons, comics, and anime. Ever-evolving stock virtually guarantees that one visit is not enough – there's always something new. Loyal customers return weekly to make sure they don't miss anything. Celebrities are spotted occasionally, hunting for new additions to their collections.

Besides worldwide imports, most from Japan and Hong Kong, the shop also carries the latest in domestic toys. An impressive array of rare and vintage collectibles are on display – and squeals of delight are often heard when someone discovers an especially nostalgic treasure. Among Toy Tokyo's most popular attractions are their extensive Godzilla collection and Bearbrick figures in various sizes. And kids, ages two to eighty-two, will find their favorites among Superheroes, GI Joes, Smurfs, Care Bears, Spiderman, Star Wars, Transformers, Urban Vinyl, and Muppets.

Toy Tokyo is the go-to shop to get very cool toys for home or office – maybe even gifts for the kids. For a real New York experience, away from touristy destinations, head to the East Village – where you can always go play with your new toy in a local park.

Toys & collectibles from around the
TOY
TOKYO!

Address 91 Second Avenue (near 5th Street), New York 10003, Phone +1 212.673.5424,
www.toytokyo.com, customerservice@toytokyo.com | Transit Subway: Astor Pl (6);
2nd Ave (F), Bus: M1, M2, M3, M8, M15, M21, M101, M102, M103 | Hours
Sun–Thurs 1–9pm, Fri–Sat 12:30–9pm

104__ Trash and Vaudeville

Take a walk on the wild side

Opened in 1975, when punk was pummeling its way into permanence, Trash and Vaudeville became one of the earliest counterculture clothing shops in the city. Mirroring the rock musician image, the shop has been setting trends for four decades. Catering to what the *New York Times* called "disenfranchised rock fans and fashion insiders," it also attracted anyone who just wanted to walk on the wild side. Born out of the 1970s rock and punk scene on St. Marks Place, the store was a favorite of the Ramones, the Heartbreakers, Blondie, the Dead Boys, and other superstar celebs.

In a funky old tenement building, it retains that grungy rundown East Village look associated with wall graffiti and stoner culture. Browse through racks of studded leather, skull pants with chains, shelves of messaged tees, clunky boots, biker vests, ripped and dyed baggies, skin-tight pants, and endless stud, glitz, and chain accessories – all screaming with in-your-face attitude.

As a teenager, owner Ray Goodman was drawn to the energy surge on that block. Whatever the scene – beatniks, hippies, glam, punk – it was all going down on St. Marks. Iconic music venues like Electric Circus, Fillmore East, and CBGB's were all within a few blocks, inspiring Goodman to open a style emporium so influenced by rock 'n' roll that it exalted the musicians themselves. Their autograph wall is like a museum piece and is worth the trip in itself. Manager/buyer Jimmy Webb, with his bleachy shag do, all-over tattoos and hand-stitched one-of-a-kinds, is the face of Trash and Vaudeville, and proud to say it's his "drug of choice."

Trash and Vaudeville's energy still flows. Frequented by rebels, street people, tattooed stoners, and dropouts, it also appeals to shoppers looking for something different. In this volcanic environment they feel transported to another space, another lifestyle – both classic and new, but always somehow rock 'n' roll.

Address 4 St. Marks Place (near Third Avenue), New York 10003, Phone +1 212.982.3590, www.trashandvaudeville.com, customerservice@trashandvaudeville.com | Transit Subway: Astor Pl (6); 8 St-NYU (N, R), Bus: M 8, M 15, M 101, M 102, M 103 | Hours Mon–Thurs 12–8pm, Fr 11:30am–8:30pm, Sat 11:30am–9pm, Sun 1–7:30pm

105 _ Twig Terrariums
Message in a bottle

Plants in glass vessels are nothing new. The Greeks grew them in bell-shaped jars 2,500 years ago. In the 1830s a botanist enclosed specimens in glass, published *On the Growth of Plants in Closely Glazed Cases*, and started a style trend in Victorian homes. The 1970s back-to-the-earth cultural movement once again revived this zen-like art form.

Fast forward to today's unique terrarium boutique in Brooklyn – aptly named Twig – the brainchild of two school chums who reunited as playful adults to create miniature plant worlds inside glass containers of various shapes and sizes: recycled vats, water-cooler bottles, lab beakers, covered cake stands, apothecary jars, gumball machines, teacups, light bulbs – the more unusual, the more interesting. Each terrarium depicts a unique environment, many with tiny figurines to create a quiet and curious voyeurism, from idyllic country scenes to quirky personal experiences based on real or imagined stories and photos. No two are exactly alike.

The scenes, delicately laid out with greenery, range from pastoral to pop to pathological – grazing sheep, a woman practicing yoga, a parachutist hung up in a tree, a couple making love in the bushes, a prison escape, a mugging in Central Park. The result is a living, breathing, 3-D snapshot of a moment frozen in time, often with an irreverent twist.

To succeed, terrariums need layers of drainage (stones), filtration (charcoal, moss), and soil. Then add plants. Building a basic terrarium doesn't require much gardening know-how and once it reaches a state of equilibrium – the right amount of moisture – it can more or less sustain itself. At Twig you can buy one readymade, design and create one with their DIY kit, or join one of their popular workshops. So learn, laugh, and enjoy the weird irony of having a perfectly landscaped, idyllic mini-world featuring an axe murderer or a zombie!

Address 287 Third Avenue (near Carroll Street), Brooklyn 11215, **Phone** +1 718.488.8944, www.twigterrariums.com, info@twigterrariums.com | **Transit** Subway: Union St (R), Bus: B 37, B 63, B 103 | **Hours** Thurs – Sun 12 – 7pm

106 Uncle Sam's Army Navy Outfitters

Atten-shun! Authentic military fashion

What's the fascination with *militaria?* A survey of today's urban scene suggests that combat mode occupies a strategic spot in the American wardrobe. Some wear fighting gear as an anti-war statement. Others flaunt their stripes to signal patriotic fervor. Still others simply make a fashion statement, no ideology. Savvy stylists go to Uncle Sam's to dress photo shoots, runway shows, movie and theater costuming, and themed events.

Uncle Sam's is the real deal. Sidestep the faux surplus shops with Timberlands and factory-distressed Levi's. Uncle Sam's is a trip through twentieth-century military history. Buying and re-selling genuine government-surplus goods worldwide since the store was founded in 1969, they purchase directly from military branches in dozens of countries. It's the go-to source for any BDU (Battle Dress Uniform) clothing. Their vast inventory is stored in Buffalo, NY, in a massive 400,000-square-foot warehouse – designed, incidentally, by Frank Lloyd Wright.

At the Greenwich Village flagship store, you can find a Vietnam War backpack (soldier's nametag sewn in), or the flight jacket of a British RAF pilot. The assortment, ever-changing, is always interesting: camo bathing suits, head-hugging *ushankas* (Russian ear-flapped fur caps), personalized dog tags, beat-up belts, real Navy pea coats, pepper spray. Get yourself an FBI t-shirt for a few bucks or a brass-buttoned Royal Canadian dress coat for a few hundred. And the help has been called "insanely attentive."

Their outfits have graced the pages of *GQ, Rolling Stone, FHM,* and *Seventeen.* The flow of celeb shoppers has included Bill Clinton, Calvin Klein, Michael Jackson, Kevin Bacon, Bono, Pink, P Diddy, 50 Cent, Billy Zane, and the gals of *Sex and the City.* None of whom would care to be seen in a pair of imitation cargos!

Address 37 West 8th Street (near Sixth Avenue), New York 10011, Phone
+1 212.674.2222, www.armynavydeals.com, dani@armynavydeals.com | Transit Subway:
West 4 St (A, B, C, D, E, F, M); Christopher St-Sheridan Sq (1); 8 St-NYU (N, R);
Astor Pl (6), Bus: M 1, M 2, M 3, M 5, M 8 | Hours Mon–Thurs 10am–8pm, Fri–Sat
10am–9pm, Sun 11am–8pm

107 ___ United Nude

Not your grandmother's shoe store

Esquire magazine dubbed Bond Street an "architectural battle-ground." On its two short cobblestoned blocks, ultra-luxury residences have sprung up in industrial-age loft buildings alongside wildly creative postmodern structures designed by world-renowned architects. The block between Lafayette and Bowery is a delightful eyeful, where graffiti meets glamour, attracting the coolest clientele (and celebs) to Noho's chicest shops.

Outstanding among them is United Nude, a stunning black cave of a store with an undulating Wall of Light that features their own architectural wonders in the guise of shoes. With futuristic footwear inspired by design principles of classics like Eames chairs, Mobius strips, and Mother Nature, some of their most intriguing styles look impossible to actually wear – until you try them on. Provocative and sensual, they're improbably comfortable – considering the extreme fashion statement they make. UN hires brazen, rule-shattering international designers to introduce innovative ideas. One soft vinyl metallic style resembles a cantilevered slinky toy. An award-winning sculptured sandal elegantly wraps the foot in one continuous strip, inspired by a mathematical shape. The queen of outrageous, Lady Gaga, asked UN to design a pair of 12-inch high heels to launch her new perfume.

Co-founder and creative director is Rem D. Koolhaas, nephew of the famed elder Dutch architect. Combining his talents with shoe designer Galahad Clark, their design firm tests the boundaries of fashion through technology. Their use of 3-D printing to make products is cutting edge. Ask about the shiny black faux-Lamborghini in the window and get an education in lo-res tech.

United Nude is perfectly positioned on this amazing street to wage architectural warfare, and is proud to proclaim: "We broke the rules of conventional shoes not for the sake of breaking them, but simply by not knowing them."

Address 25 Bond Street (near Lafayette), New York 10012, Phone +1 212.420.6000, www.unitednude.com | **Transit** Subway: Bleecker St (6); Broadway-Lafayette (B, D, F, M); Prince St (N, R), Bus: M 1, M 2, M 5, M 8, M 15, M 21, M 103 | **Hours** Sun–Mon 12–7pm, Tue–Thurs 11am–7pm, Fri–Sat 11am–8pm

108___Village Tannery
Art of the leather bag

The rich smell of fine leather and deliciously inviting colors welcome you to the Village Tannery. On a relatively secluded street in Noho, this exclusive leather shop produces designs you may have admired in passing, but perhaps never considered their true artistic value. Here, surrounded by bags of all sizes, shapes, and styles, you marvel at just that. Old-world craftsmanship using the best quality hides produces some of the most original bags available in a vivid palette of colors, textures, and patterns.

Talented Turkish-American designer Sevestet has established herself as one of today's recognized leather innovators. Her experienced artisans can be glimpsed carefully cutting and stitching each piece individually in the open workshop at the back of the shop. These craftsmen begin as apprentices, watching and learning techniques from masters. Each item is lovingly handcrafted – some into popular styles, other creations completely unique.

The shop is a forest of backpacks, handbags, clutches, hobo bags, totes, briefcases, duffles, carry-ons, fanny-packs, saddlebags, or cases to coddle your iPad. You can bring in your own idea for a design, or even a buckle for a belt to be custom-made for you. Prices go as high as $1,000, but the range of choices is from affordable to extravagant. Proof of Village Tannery's pride and confidence is its policy of offering a lifetime labor warranty.

One customer brought in a weekend duffle bag for repair that he'd bought twenty-one years before. The shop fixed it for free, then generously offered to replace it with a new one. The customer refused, saying he loved his timeworn bag more than ever. Of course.

A single bag does not a tannery make. But they believe that each individual bag is "a triumph of our soul and spirit." You're buying years of skill and tradition, an ageless and wondrous piece of work. You're buying art.

Address 7 Great Jones Street (near Broadway), New York 10012, Phone +1 212.979.0013, www.villagetannery.com, villagetannery@aol.com | Transit Subway: Bleecker St (6); Broadway-Lafayette (B, D, F, M), Bus: M1, M2, M5, M8, M21, M103 | Hours Mon–Sat 11am–7pm, Sun 12–6pm

109__Vintage Thrift Shop

A hunting expedition in grandma's attic

Small spaces can be a challenge, but they can also be a triumph. The modest size of this Gramercy shop forces a level of curating that's usually reserved for high-end boutiques but is rarely seen on the thrift-shop circuit, where prices are notably low-end. Lining this cozy space from floor to ceiling you'll find a cornucopian trove of functional and stylish housewares, furniture, artwork, books, music, jewelry, clothing, and accessories.

While the selection is first-rate, this is no pretentious, hands-off museum. Customers are free to touch and try on just about everything here. The staff knows their stuff and will happily share history and details about unusual *objets*. Almost every item at Vintage is 'a real find' – one reason it has earned Best Thrift Shop status from discriminating *Zagat's NYC Shopping Guide* for seven years in a row.

Whimsical displays are a point of pride for this eclectic emporium, with window items going on the auction block every several weeks. Among the exceptional goodies sold at auction in the past: a set of six mint-condition Donghia chairs; stunning collections of Jadeite, Fiestaware, and Bakelite; and an antique gramophone (that sparked quite a bidding war).

Every item in the store has been donated, with all proceeds going to nonprofits helping the needy on the Lower East Side. The shop's array of practical and collectible merchandise attracts a loyal following of customers and donors alike – many celebrities among them – keeping it well-stocked with a constant turnover of quality surprises. So abundant is the wealth of donations, they opened a jewel-box boutique in the West Village catering to a fashion-oriented clientele, featuring secondhand designer pieces and one-of-a-kind vintage apparel. Whether you are on a hunt for inspiration, for a unique gift, or on a serious mission for collectibles, expect to be delighted to find something unexpected.

Address 286 Third Avenue (at 22nd Street), New York 10010, Phone +1 212.871.0777, www.vintagethriftshop.org | **Transit** Subway: 23 St (6, N, R), Bus: M 1, M 2, M 3, M 9, M 15, M 23, M 101, M 102, M 103 | **Hours** Mon–Thurs 10:30am–8pm, Fri 10:30am–dusk, Sun 11am–7pm

110 Whiskers Holistic Pet Care

No pet peeves here!

Welcome to the brave new age of alternative pet care. This eye-popping storefront is as unconventional as the services provided by Phil and Randy Klein, who founded it in 1988. Their mission is to bring the benefits of holistic wellness to the universe of companion animals – cats, dogs, birds, fish, and most other lovable, domesticated creatures. How that type of animal lived in the wild is Whiskers' model for their health, because nature knows best. Their success is based on highly selective products and practices – herbs, vitamins, supplements, customized diets, cleansers, raw foods, skin care, and natural treats. Maybe quirky, but proven effective.

Desperate pet owners, frustrated with conventional veterinary solutions to their furry companions' persistent problems, consult the dedicated staff of self-described 'animal crazies' who dispense advice on organic foods, homeopathic and herbal remedies. "The worst that can happen," they're quick to say, "is that nothing happens."

Leaf through the albums brimming with expressions of gratitude and accolades from satisfied customers. Their success is largely based on enlightenment and education of pet owners about alternatives to mainstream practices that have a pharmaceutical approach. The shop regularly hosts free events such as food presentations, veterinary consultations, and pet rescue events.

A true community gathering place, pet owners come in to get trusted recommendations for cat-sitters, dog-walkers, obedience trainers, and animal psychologists. There are oodles of non-toxic toys and treats, pet apparel, and specially prepared fresh food for home cooking. It's refreshing to find a store so committed to its beliefs, practices, and products that keep our cherished animal friends healthy and happy. Whiskers' cage-free Rescue Cat Ranch shelters adorable homeless kittens just pining to be taken into a loving heart and home. Come in and just feel the love.

Address 235 East 9th Street (near Second Avenue), New York 10003, Phone +1 212.979.2532, www.1800whiskers.com, healthypet@msn.com | Transit Subway: Astor Pl (6); 8 St-NYU (N, R), Bus: M1, M3, M8, M15, M102, M103 | Hours Mon–Fri 11am–8pm, Sat 11am–7pm, Sun 12–6pm

111__ Yonah Schimmel Knish Bakery

A nostalgic nosh

Yonah Schimmel's describes itself as the oldest knishery in America. When people ask current owner Ellen Anistratov if her knishes are fresh, she tells them, "They're a hundred years old," attesting to the resiliency of the bakery which opened at its present site in 1910. Today it sits anachronistically between a cinema and a trendy hotel on East Houston Street. Schimmel was an Eastern European Jewish immigrant who began vending his wife's knishes from a pushcart on the Lower East Side in the 1890s. A few years later, he and his cousin opened their shop on Houston Street.

No one knows for certain when and where the knish was inspired. But for the uninitiated, a knish is a thin dough shell filled with either mashed-up (not whipped) potatoes or kasha (buckwheat groats) mixed with chopped onion. Beyond that, knishes may also be filled with ingredients as far-ranging as blueberry- or cherry- or broccoli-cheese, spinach, and cabbage. Over the years, Schimmel's has created a host of other fillings. The most important thing is freshness – never fast-frozen, mass produced, deep-fried, or otherwise Americanized. Schimmel's recipe uses no oil, eggs, or yeast. They are hand-shaped into round fist-sized treats in the basement kitchen, then oven-baked and hoisted up – hot and steaming – to the ground-floor shop by a rope on a pulley in the building's original dumbwaiter. This old fossil of a contraption is an attraction in itself.

The knishery has attracted a long list of famous figures during its century-long history – from the Marx Brothers to Larry David. The walls are plastered with recognizable faces in yellowing photographs and old newspaper clippings. In recent years, the ethnicity of the Lower East Side has changed and most of the stores from the old days are gone. But Schimmel's fourth-generation owner has a slogan to suit the times: *One World, One Taste, One Knish.*

Address 137 East Houston Street (near Forsyth Street), New York 10002, **Phone** +1 212.477.2858, www.yonahschimmel.com | **Transit** Subway: 2nd Ave (F), **Bus:** M 15, M 21, M 103 | **Hours** Daily 9am –7pm

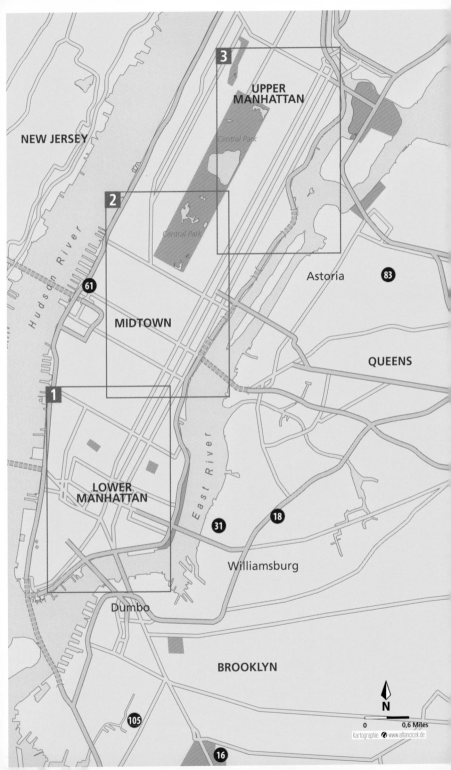

Jo-Anne Elikann
**111 PLACES IN NEW YORK
THAT YOU MUST NOT MISS**
ISBN 978-3-95451-052-8

Gordon Streisand
**111 PLACES IN MIAMI AND THE
KEYS THAT YOU MUST NOT MISS**
ISBN 978-3-95451-644-5

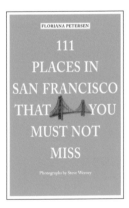

Floriana Petersen
**111 PLACES IN SAN FRANCISCO
THAT YOU MUST NOT MISS**
ISBN 978-3-95451-609-4

Sally Asher, Michael Murphy
**111 PLACES IN NEW ORLEANS
THAT YOU MUST NOT MISS**
ISBN 978-3-95451-645-2

Desa Philadelphia
**111 SHOPS IN LOS ANGELES
THAT YOU MUST NOT MISS**
ISBN 978-3-95451-615-5

Kirstin von Glasow
**111 SHOPS IN LONDON THAT YOU
SHOULDN'T MISS**
ISBN 978-3-95451-341-3

Kirstin von Glasow
**111 COFFEESHOPS IN LONDON
THAT YOU MUST NOT MISS**
ISBN 978-3-95451-614-8

John Sykes
**111 PLACES IN LONDON THAT YOU
SHOULDN'T MISS**
ISBN 978-3-95451-346-8

Lucia Jay von Seldeneck, Carolin Huder,
Verena Eidel
**111 PLACES IN BERLIN THAT YOU
SHOULDN'T MISS**
ISBN 978-3-95451-208-9

Rüdiger Liedtke
**111 PLACES IN MUNICH THAT YOU
SHOULDN'T MISS**
ISBN 978-3-95451-222-5

Peter Eickhoff
**111 PLACES IN VIENNA THAT YOU
SHOULDN'T MISS**
ISBN 978-3-95451-206-5

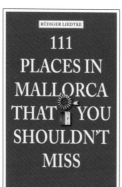

Rüdiger Liedtke
**111 PLACES IN MALLORCA THAT
YOU SHOULDN'T MISS**
ISBN 978-3-95451-281-2

Acknowledgements

With sincere thanks to our German team: Achim Mantscheff, Monika Elisa Schurr, Constanze Keutler, Gerd Wiechcinski; and to our US team: Sudha Dunienville, John Brancati, Sean Nam, Sara Guenoun, Jen Burch. With gratitude to our friends for helpful suggestions: Jo-Anne Elikann, Arthur Levin, Lena Tabori, Joost Elffers, Theo Jeuken, Robert Tamburino. Special thanks to Andreas Landshoff, who graciously introduced us to this project. And of course, with love to our children Jeremy Lusk and Julia Gabor for their moral support.

The authors

Susan Lusk has been an art director, book editor, photographer and indie publisher. She's been taking pictures since her dad gave her his old Leica when she was a kid. She has a degree in fine arts, and has always lived, loved, and shopped in New York – the center of the universe.

Mark Gabor has been a freelance writer and editor for over 30 years. Raised in the historic neighborhood of Hell's Kitchen, his love for New York has kept him exploring the city's streets since he was a youngster. He has lived in Soho and the East Village, and now resides in Greenwich Village. He is constantly on the lookout for new stores in the city – a pastime with no possible end in sight!